GOD *and the ways of knowing*

translated by Walter Roberts

Meridian Books

THE WORLD PUBLISHING COMPANY

Cleveland and New York

JEAN DANIÉLOU

GOD

and

the

ways

of

knowing

Translated from the original French text, Dieu et Nous.

A MERIDIAN BOOK

Published by The World Publishing Company
2231 West 110th Street, Cleveland 2, Ohio

First printing (as a Meridian Greenwich Editions original)
   August 1957
Second printing (as a Meridian Books edition) July 1960
Fifth printing September 1963
Library of Congress Catalog Card Number: 57-10853
Typography and design by Elaine Lustig
Printed in the United States of America   5WP963

Nihil obstat
John A. Goodwine, J.C. D. / Censor Librorum

Imprimatur
✠ Francis Cardinal Spellman/Archbishop of New York

foreword

Origen used to say that it is always dangerous to speak of God. It is true that all we say of Him seems utterly unworthy, in comparison with what He is; and accordingly we fear that what we say may conceal more than it reveals of His nature, and may be more of a hindrance than a help. We should wish, too, after everything we have said, to say the opposite. Because at one and the same time it seems that all we say of Him is true, and also untrue; for He is what we say, and yet He is not. He is, as Pseudo-Dionysus observes, all that is and nothing that is.

Is it even necessary to speak of God? For if He is always unknown, He is also, paradoxically, well-known. Why speak of Him as if one knew Him better than others, since everyone knows Him? For nothing is better known than God. No other being than He occupies so large a place in the life even of those who deny Him, or believe that they do not know Him. Emmanuel Berl said recently that he had never met an atheist, only men who believe in God, without knowing exactly what they believe. So God is the most known and the most unknown. A little child knows Him, perhaps before knowing its mother, and the greatest mystics do not know Him.

If, notwithstanding, it is possible to speak of God, it is only because God has spoken of Himself. As Barth says: "Only God speaks of God." My plan in this book is, then, not to record what I say of God, but what God has said of Himself. This is what justifies my plan and provides its directive. For God has spoken several times. He spoke and He speaks to all men through Creation, which is His handiwork, and through the spirit, which is His image. Then He spoke by His Prophets. And finally He spoke by His Son. Thus it is the same God who made Himself known to the heathen and to the philosophers, to the Jews and to the Christians. But amid all these ways of knowing God, it is desirable to establish some kind of order. And that is really the aim of this book: to place religions and philosophies, the Old Testament and the New, theology and mysticism, in their proper relationship with the knowledge of God.

In this book we should also wish to help those who are groping after God, by showing them the ways by which He makes Himself known. We should wish to guide those who know God, by explaining to them how He reveals Himself in many ways, and yet how His revelation in Jesus Christ is pre-eminent and definitive. We should wish to help Christians to place within their knowledge of God the many ways that are offered to them, to love the Bible without depreciating theology, and to study theology without neglecting mysticism. We should wish above all, in a world from which God seems so absent, to restore the progressive stages by which He manifests Himself, and by which He can be rediscovered.

GOD *and the ways of knowing*

I

THE GOD OF
the religions

The first sign of the meeting between God and man
is that of the pagan religions. It is first chronologi-
cally, in that biblical religion begins, strictly speaking, with Abraham. It is first also in application,
in that it is the first general form of religion. I
use here the term "pagan religion," in preference
to that of "natural religion," to designate this
datum in its concrete reality, that of the whole
assembly of non-biblical religions. Those religions
are not natural, first of all, in that they do not
express the revelation of God through nature in the
pure state, but are always elaborations. They are
not natural either in another sense, insofar as they
are historically those of men who find themselves
in a world which from its very beginning is a
world of grace and sin.

The position of these religions within a Christian
perspective poses a difficult problem which has
scarcely been broached.[1] We may say that the view
of the man in the street is much too broad. For
many men of our time, these religions are not to be
radically distinguished from biblical religions. Es-

tablishing multiple analogies between Christian and pagan rites and doctrines, historians of religion often see in Christianity a phase in the religious evolution of mankind, and subordinate it to the history of religion, of which it would constitute a branch. Religious persons, struck by the inward experience to which, in particular, the higher religions of the East bear witness, seek there for spiritual food, quite as much as among Christian authors, and see in the various religions, including Christianity, various forms of the "transcendental unity" of religion.

We utterly reject such evolutionary and syncretist theories. Christianity cannot, any more than Judaism, be described as a manifestation of an immanent evolution of the religious genius of mankind, of which these two are merely the relatively higher expressions. They are interventions in history of a transcendent God who introduces man into a domain which is radically closed to him. In this sense one can, with Guardini, oppose revelation and religion. The Bible bears witness to a revelation of God addressed to men of all religions.

Besides, the problem is not that of knowing whether we find among non-Christian religions a religious experience as rich as that which we find in Christianity. An aptitude for religion is a human datum. It can exist alike among non-Christians as among Christians. Buddha and Mohammed are greater religious geniuses than St. Peter or the Curé d'Ars. But that which saves is not religious experience, but faith in the Word of God. As Guardini has well said, "We are not great religious personalities, we are servants of the Word." The question is of knowing whether a means of salvation is given in Jesus Christ, and of believing in Him.

The assimilation of Christianity to the non-Christian religions is therefore an unfortunate confusion. For all that, should we condemn these religions without a hearing? This is the view that we find in primitive Christianity. Men as well disposed towards the classic philosophers as Clement of Alexandria are yet astonishingly hard on pagan religions. We find this view again today in orthodox Protestantism, perhaps in reaction against liberal Protestantism and its syncretism. For Karl Barth, the God of the pagan religions is an idol forged by man, in which he worships himself; it must be entirely destroyed to make room for the revelation of Jesus Christ, who alone is God's work. Hendrick Kraemer applies this Barthian position to missionary theology, and regards paganism as a mere obstacle which must be entirely replaced by faith in Jesus Christ.

Catholic tradition, especially in the last hundred years, has maintained a less negative position, which is moreover the outcome of her idea of a human nature spoiled by sin, but not utterly perverted. She does indeed uncompromisingly condemn the perversions which, without exception, are presented by all the pagan religions, idolatry, pantheism, Manichaeism, and so forth. She regards them, too, as having been outmoded, ever since a higher truth was manifested in Christ. But for all that, she does not deny that authentic religious values are found in them, signs of that help which God has never ceased to give man, stepping-stones related to Judaism and to Christianity. "God," says St. Paul in *The Acts of the Apostles,* "who in times past suffered all nations to walk in their own ways. Nevertheless he left not himself without testimony, doing good from heaven, giving rains and fruitful season, filling our hearts with food and gladness."[2]

It must be added that the works of historians of religion, in particular those of Georges van der Leeuw and Mircéa Eliade, have lent support to this traditional Christian position. Indeed, a better understanding of doctrines and rites which at first glance might seem to be signs of degraded superstition, has shown that very often they were signs of a genuine religion. When pagans worship the god of the sun or the storm, they are not always offering their devotion to physical phenomena. These appear to them, in Eliade's phrase, as hierophanies, as manifestations of a mysterious power, and it is this that they worship through its appearance.[3] Certainly it is sometimes difficult to see how much idolatry or polytheism may be mingled with these beliefs. They are almost always contaminated. But this does not exclude a certain knowledge and worship of the true God.

How, then, are we to explain these values in the pagan religions? That is a question which involves the theological status of the history of religion, the place of the history of religion in the history of salvation. For such is the only correct way of posing the problem from a Christian standpoint. The ancient Fathers of the Church had already encountered this difficulty, and they gave a preliminary answer with their theory of "borrowings." The truths of the pagan religions were regarded as loans drawn upon revelation, whether from Moses or from the Gospel. Whatever such influences there may be, it is clear that this interpretation is, in the main, unacceptable. Besides, to prove it the Fathers were forced to base their argument on arbitrary chronological surmises.

The doctrine commonly accepted in the nineteenth century, and chiefly connected with Lamenais, is that of primitive revelation. The truths of the pagan religions were regarded as the remains of the positive revelation made to Adam in the earthly paradise. Fr. Schmidt in our time has tried to give this theory a scientific justification, by basing his argument on the connection which he claims to have found between the primitive character of a culture and the purity of its religion. But this theory has not withstood the measured criticism of Van der Leeuw.[4] Whatever survival there may be of primitive revelation—which indeed is attested by the Bible—it is difficult to link it to all the scattered and separated truths which the various religions present. The continuity of primitive tradition across the tens of millennia of human history between Adam and Abraham is impossible to establish.

Besides, Scripture itself directs us towards another solution. The Old Testament declares on many occasions that apart from any positive revelation God

shows Himself to all men through His providence
in the world of nature. "The heavens declare the
glory of God," exclaims the Psalmist (19:1);
and he continues: "There is not a word nor a discourse whose voice is not heard: Through all the
earth their voice resounds, and to the ends of the
world, their message" (19: 3-4). There is, then, a
word that God speaks to the whole earth through
the visible world. That is why it is only the fool
who "says in his heart, 'There is no God.'" [5] *The
Book of Job* describes in a stately manner this
cosmic manifestation of God (38-39); and *Genesis*
gives us its justification by showing us, in the regular pattern of the cosmic cycles, the courses of the
stars and the sequence of the seasons, a sign of
God's faithfulness to the promise He made to
Noah. [6]

The Old Testament bears witness also that men,
who did not belong to Israel by race or religion—
and so were what we call heathen—knew and
reverenced the true God. Thus Noah, raising an altar
after the Flood, finds favor in the sight of God,
according to the Scriptures, by means of this offering. Thus Enoch, who walked with God [7]; thus
Melchizedek, priest of *El Elyon,* of God Almighty,
whose sacrifice is presented in the liturgy of the
Mass as a foreshadowing of the sacrifice of Christ;
thus Lot, the nephew of Abraham, but a stranger
to his religion, whom the Christians of the country of Moab revered as a saint in the fourth century, and whose name is forever inscribed in the
martyrology; thus the Queen of Sheba, of whom

Christ said that she would judge the unfaithful Jews on the last day; thus Job himself, the venerable sage of Idumaea, whom the sacred author presents to us as a pagan, and whom nevertheless he makes the pattern of true religion.[8]

The New Testament makes this doctrine more precise, and in proclaiming the good news to the pagans, shows them that God has never abandoned them, and that it is just because of this that they are to blame for not having believed in Him. The *Acts of the Apostles* show us St. Paul saying to the Athenians: "God hath made of one, all mankind to dwell upon the whole face of the earth, determining appointed times, and the limits of their habitation. That they should seek God, if happily they may feel after him, or find him, although he be not far from every one of us."[9] God's providence reaches out, therefore, to every race; and through Providence, all men can reach up to the knowledge of God. But they feel after Him without the help of a positive revelation. That is why their ideas of Him are vague and confused.[10]

Already to the pagans of Lystra, who sought to worship Him, Paul had given a similar teaching: "the living God, who made the heaven, and the earth, and the sea, and all things that are in them. Who in times past suffered all nations to walk in their own ways . . . left not himself without testimony, doing good from heaven, giving rains and fruitful seasons, filling our hearts with food and gladness."[11] The evidence that God continually offers of Himself among the nations is to be found in the regularity of rain and harvest, of which we have said that it was the object of the cosmic covenant; and it is remarkable that in fact the basis of pagan religion should be the knowledge of God through the rhythms of nature, expressed liturgically by the cycle of seasonal feasts.

The *Epistle to the Romans* maintains still more strongly this manifestation of the invisible God through His visible works: "For the invisible things of him, from the creation of the world, are clearly seen, being understood by the things that are made" (1:20). Paul insists on the responsibility men who "when they knew God, they have glorified him as God, or given thanks; but . . . changed the glory of the incorruptible God into the likeness of the image of a corruptible man, and of birds, and of fourfooted beasts, and of creeping things." (1:21, 23).

Thus idolatry is a culpable degradation of that cosmic revelation by which man could attain to the knowledge of the true God. Such is, moreover, the doctrine which the Vatican Council solemnly reaffirmed against traditionalist and fideist errors, by declaring that the knowledge of God is accessible to all men.[12]

The *Epistle to the Romans* adds a new idea of great importance when it states that God reveals Himself not only through the voice of the visible world, but also through that of the moral conscience: "For when the Gentiles who have not the law, do by nature those things that are of the law, these, having not the law, are a law to themselves: who shew the work of the Lord written in their hearts, their conscience bearing witness to them." [13] So there are not only the Tables given to Moses on Sinai; the divine will is also graven upon the table of the heart by the finger of God, which is the Spirit. Through the absolute of the moral law, man can recognize the existence and nature of Him, who alone can command absolute obedience in such a way that obedience to the moral law expresses the worship of the will.

From all these biblical testimonies there emerges a doctrine of the nature of pagan religions. Before He spoke through Moses and through Jesus Christ God spoke to all men through the cosmos and the conscience. St. Paul states formally that the pagan religions are the outcome of this first revelation. But since they are received by a humanity whose intellect and conscience are marred by the consequences of original sin—a humanity which has neither the outward support of a positive revelation nor the inward help of an effective grace, without however being deprived of all supernatural aid— this revelation finds difficulty in penetrating souls with its full integrity. Since they are capable of receiving it, that is why some souls have managed to grasp it and why the deviations of others are to be blamed. The fact is that man seeks after it and is almost always lost, so that the pagan religions are like rays of cosmic revelation, refracted through a humanity spoiled by sin and not yet enlightened by positive revelation. This explains why, in Emil Brunner's phrase, error is always mingled with truth.

Besides, this cosmic revelation, of which the pagan religions are defective signs, is in every way an imperfect, incomplete revelation. Mosaic revelation and Christian revelation infinitely surpass it. It represents a past phase in the history of revelation. This is doubtless what makes it possible to judge the pagan religions impartially. They are, above all, outmoded survivals of a period in the history of salvation which is not our own. To remain at that stage is a sin. It is in this sense that they are, at the same time, partially true and yet untrue. Buddha, Zoroaster, Confucius may be treated as forerunners of Christ. But the function of a forerunner, as Guardini has well shown, is to efface himself when he whom he is sent to introduce makes his appearance. If he fails to do so, he becomes the enemy.

Up to this point we have tried to define the status of the pagan religions within a Christian perspective. We have established that they have at the same time a positive aspect and a fundamental vagueness. It is these two aspects which we must now fathom: first, what do the pagan religions tell us about the true God? and second, what are the deep-seated ambiguities that characterize their statements about Him? We find much support here in the remarkable work that has been done on the phenomenology of religion, especially by Eliade and

Van der Leeuw, who have disentangled from the vast material accumulated particularly in the past two centuries the common structures that enable us to describe the basic forms of religion.

The first characteristic of cosmic religion is that God is known in it, as Paul said to the Romans, through visible things. The whole cosmos takes on a symbolic dimension. The realities that constitute it—the stars and the regularity of their courses, the rock and its stillness, the dew and its blessing—ar[e] so many hierophanies, visible manifestations throug[h] each of which an aspect of God is revealed. T[he] revelation has as well a metaphysical basis in [the] general analogy of being; according to this, [all?] being is a participation in God, and bears s[ome] traces of Him. The world is also a book [that] speaks to us of God; and this book was the o[nly] one available to pagan humanity.

Such symbolic knowledge has often seemed arb[i-]trary and fantastic to that modern rationalism which has been molded by the rigor of deductive reason. But the phenomenology of religion has re-stored some of its gnoseological value. On the one hand it has been noticed that the same symbols—fire, darkness, dew—always stood for similar reali-ties. It is very much a question, then, of an objec-tive relationship between the symbol and its object, and not that of a gratuitous interpretation. The symbol is the medium for a perfectly objective knowledge. Besides, Jung's depth psychology has shown how the objective value of symbolism was connected even with the structure of the spirit, because symbols express permanent intellectual and emotional content.

We can retrieve some of these hierophanies by following the work of Mircéa Eliade.[14] The sky occupies an important place in many religions, in Oceania, China, India, Iran and Greece. It appears as a sign of the supreme god. It expresses for primitive man a sense of transcendence, of the ccessible world which he can never attain. It vides, moreover, in contrast with the variability earthly things and, in particular, of the atmos- re, an immutable movement which makes it a ool of eternity. Finally, it is the mysterious ce of the d rain, the symbol of the power God the Creator.

heavenly forms, the sun occupies a place. We know the importance of sun- among the Incas as well as in Mithraism. un provided the final form of Roman pagan- . It appears as the force that puts the darkness o flight. In this sense it symbolizes divinity as the source of knowledge. But it is also the life-giving principle of the whole cosmos, and reveals God as the source of life. The hierophany of the moon, too, has a relationship with the forces of fertility. But it is still more closely connected with the chthonian forces, with the vegetable world. Its association with water and the serpent has often been noticed. Its tutelary presence signifies an aspect, different from that of the sun, of divine protection.

In every religion the storm is a prominent numinous theme. Even modern man experiences at its coming a sacred thrill, which is not merely due to the threat of danger that it represents; and the old peasant woman crosses herself at its approach. In fact the various elements in the storm—dark clouds, lightning, the crash of thunder—appear, by the terror which they inspire, as hierophanies of the divine anger, that is to say, of God's intense vitality, of the unbearable concentration of His existence, which man does not venture to approach. The prophet Habacuc describes the appearance of Yahweh by taking up this storm-symbolism:

> *"The mountains saw thee, and were*
> *grieved:*
> *The great body of water passed away:*
> *The deep put forth his voice; the deep*
> *lifted up its hands,*
> *The sun and moon stood still in their*
> *habitation,*
> *In the light of thy arrows they shall*
> *go,*
> *In the brightness of thy glittering*
> *spear."* [15]

This is not the only example of cosmic symbols being taken up into biblical revelation. It is indeed a principle of the revelational sequence that a new revelation does not destroy, but takes over the values of the previous revelation. Christ did not destroy the Law; on the contrary, He fulfilled it. So in the first instance the Law did not abolish, but rather fulfilled, cosmic religion. The Jewish festivals of Easter, Pentecost and Tabernacles replaced the ancient seasonal festivals, and the disciples of Elijah replaced the priestesses of Astarte on Carmel. Christianity itself did not scruple to celebrate on the day of the winter solstice, when the *Natale Solis invicti* was celebrated, the birth of Christ, demonstrating by this means that He was indeed the eternally rising sun of the new Creation, where, according to the Book of the *Apocalypse,* "the city hath no need of ≥ sun . . . for the glory of God hath enlightened (21 : 23).

This seems very relevant to two hierophanies of ich we have not yet spoken. The first is that of Mircéa Eliade gives a remarkable analy-ne values implied by this example: "Noth-uld be more immediate and more autonomous the fullness of its power, nothing more noble and more terrifying than the majestic rock. It reveals something that transcends the precariousness of the human situation—a mode of absolute being. Its resistance, its inertia, its proportions, even its strange contours, are not human; they bear witness to a presence that dazzles, frightens, attracts and threatens." [16]

But it is remarkable that the rock, which occupies a considerable place in pagan religion, is one of the symbols chosen in the Bible to signify God. The song of Moses in *Deuteronomy* refers to Him by this name: "The Rock, how faultless are his deeds, how right all his ways! A faithful God without deceit, how just and upright he is." (32 : 4). But in taking up this symbol the text gives it a new meaning. It signifies God's truth, *emet.* For the

Bible, this does not consist of the fact that God en-
lightens the intellect, but of the fact that He can be
leaned upon with one's whole weight. This is of supreme importance in making clear the biblical conception of truth, which does not rest on the evidence
of anything known—as it does for the Greeks, for
whom its symbol is light—but on the solidity of the
evidence that enables us to know.

Here in turn the New Testament takes up the
metaphor and applies it to Christ: "The Rock
was Christ," [17] says St. Paul. But the metaphor
takes on a new meaning which continues and surpasses the previous ones. It signifies now the very
person of Christ insofar as He is the rock on whom
rests the new creation of the Church, the unshakable
foundation-stone on which her whole structure is
based. On this bedrock the foundations of the
Apostles and the Prophets depend. Above them there
rises the mansion of the Spirit, composed of living
souls, in which the Trinity has Its dwelling: "In
whom you are also built together into an habitation
of God in the Spirit." [18]

Another symbol whose history runs parallel is that
of rain. In the pagan religions it is a sign of God's
blessing on the parched earth, a favor always de-
sired and always marvelled at, which gives life and
joy to the earth. It is associated with the nocturnal
moon which provides refreshment from the harsh
rays of the sun. But the Bible takes over this symbol to express spiritual blessings. *Et nubes pluant
iustum.*[19] In particular, it compares the lifegiving
power of rain with that of God's word:

> *"And as the rain and the snow come*
> *down from heaven,*
> *And return no more thither,*
> *But soak the earth and water it,*
> *And make it to spring,*
> *And give seed to the sower, and bread*
> *to the eater:*
> *So shall my word be, which shall go*
> *forth from my mouth."* [20]

And Pseudo-Dionysus, enumerating the names of God, can write: "He is sun, star, fire, earth, breath, dew, cloud, absolute rock, stone, in a word all that is and nothing that is." [21]

Just as cosmic religion knows God through His appearance in the world, so it pictures His action on the level of natural reality. In this context He is essentially the Lord of the cosmos, He who takes upon Himself its preservation. Man is a part of the world of nature. What he expects from God, the object of his religion, is earthly prosperity. The world of the dead appears as a mysterious, unreal halo that surrounds the sphere of cosmic life. But it is the latter that possesses sovereign reality. The expectation of another life, better than the present, arises only in certain streams of personal piety, as far as paganism is concerned. It is Christianity that confers on it a pre-eminent value.

This relationship between God and the cosmos is revealed at the same time in the myth that explains it and in the ritual that makes it work. The myth is the normal form, on the level of cosmic religion, of the expression of God's relation to the world. It consists in the affirmation of the existence, in a world of archetypes, of the patterns of all human realities. These archetypes are the immutable models in which every reality participates. They have their being in what Van der Leeuw calls primordial or mythical time, which is abstracted from the changeability of concrete time.[22] In that realm the gods and heroes perform eternal acts which men repeat. Men's actions are only real insofar as they faithfully reproduce these pre-existing patterns.

Such myths comprise the "theology" of cosmic religions. The majority of them are cosmogonic myths which have for their object the generation of the world: among the Australian aborigines we find the myth of the cosmic egg that contains the whole of creation; among the Babylonian religions we find the myth of Marduk and Tiamat, the sungod and the dragon of the abyss, whose cosmic struggle expresses the triumph of light and order over chaos, the primitive *tohuv'bohu* of the Hebrews; in ancient Greece we find the myth of Kronos, killed by his son Saturn, giving birth through his seed to the life of mankind. It is not a question here of causal explanations in the manner which the Greek philosophers attempted, when they applied their newly-invented scientific method to metaphysical realities; neither is it a question of the paradoxical revelation of creation, such as the Bible proclaims. But, according to the mythological process, it is a matter of perceiving a correspondence between a pre-existing world, whose origin and nature are not in question, and the world of here and now.

However, the myths do not only have a bearing on the primal origin of things. All the essential realities of life, the cultivation of the earth and the pursuit of game, the work of the weaver and the smith, the first moments of the new-born child and the onset of puberty, marriage and child-birth, death and burial, in a word, the whole of human life in its most permanent features is abstracted from the profane world. It possesses in mythical time the sacred archetypes of which it is part. For in the mythical world the gods and heroes have achieved for all eternity the typical acts of work, love, war and death.[23] That is why the myths repeat these fabulous exploits which so resemble those of men; but human exploits are only their pale reflection.

The problem of the relationship between cosmic myth and biblical revelation poses, in an acute form, the question of the relationship between Christianity and paganism. For some, the Christian mysteries are not fundamentally different from those of the cosmic myths. Already Porphyry and Celsus make a close comparison between the virgin birth of Christ and the miraculous births of mythology, between the resurrection of Christ and that of Adonis. Modern syncretism has revived these parallels. Simone Weil, in her *Letter to a Priest*, amasses the similarities between the vine of Dionysus and that of St. John, between the Cross of Christ and the cosmic tree.[24] To avoid such assimilation, Rudolf Bultmann seeks, in a violent reaction, to demythologize Christianity, by recognizing that the pictures in which it is expressed are indeed myths, whether it is a question of the Incarnation, the Resurrection or the Last Judgment, and that faith is an act of allegiance to the salvation given by Jesus Christ, beyond all pictorial representations.

In reality the problem arises in much the same way as that of symbolism. Christian biblical revelation owes nothing to myths. It deals with unique divine acts, unprecedented and unfounded in human life. The veneration of Mary is not, as Jung claims, that of the feminine element in divinity, like the virgin mothers of Hellenism or Hinduism, but it rests exclusively on her rôle at a unique moment in the history of salvation. The Cross of Christ is not the cosmic symbol of the four dimensions, but the wretched gibbet on which the Savior of the world was hanged. The vine is not the symbol of Dionysian immortality, but that of the people of Israel planted by Yahweh. The resurrection is not the expression of the cyclical triumph of life over death in the spring of every year, but the unique event which, once for all, introduced man into the sphere of the life of the Trinity.[25]

In this connection we may note that one of the most characteristic contrasts between cosmic and biblical religion is that, in the first, God manifests Himself through the regularity of seasonal cycles, while in the second He reveals Himself in the uniqueness of historical events. Cosmic religion is bound up with permanent patterns. For it, the historical and the unique are unreal; only what is repeated has value. Biblical revelation, on the contrary, places us in the presence of new, decisive divine acts which modify the human situation in a definite way and are not to be repeated. Christ died and rose again once on behalf of all. Adonis, the symbol of biological life, dies every autumn and is reborn every spring. It is with Christianity that time assumes a value as the locus where a divine plan is worked out.

Thus the mythological character that Bultmann believes he has brought to light in the Christian mysteries is alien to their substance. But it remains true that these events, which in their origin owe nothing to myths, were often expressed afterwards in pictures borrowed from myths. For Christianity does not destroy these, but takes over their truth. Thus the Fathers of the Church rejoiced to unfold the symbolism of the Cross of Christ by showing in its four dimensions a sign of the universal character of redemption. Thus the resurrection of Christ, placed liturgically in the framework of the seasonal feast of the sprouting corn, seemed as if charged with all the symbolism of spring. Thus the descent of Christ into hell, which by origin signifies only the proclaiming of freedom to the saints of the Old Testament, takes on the form of a cosmic battle between Christ and the Prince of darkness.[26]

If the myth explains the relationship between God and the cosmos, the rite aims at making it work. Cosmic religions include an infinite number of rites. These are symbolic acts which are held to be charged with a *dynamis,* a hidden virtue, and to possess a mysterious efficacy. Thus a libation of water imitates

and at the same time provokes rain; the offering of
a victim signifies and sets to work an attitude of dependence upon divinity; rites of spring imitate and
set in motion a new creation of the world; immersion
in water symbolizes and activates the purification of
that which has been defiled.

These rites have been interpreted in many different ways. Christians have often seen in them magi-
cal practices designed to protect them against demonic forces. And indeed there is such a thing as
magic. But it is a degradation of cosmic religion.
Rites have also been interpreted as signs of a connection between the different parts of the cosmos,
by virtue of a universal sympathy. This sympathy
would establish an analogical causality, according to
which the ritual imitation would determine, as if
mechanically, the real effect. But this metaphysical
interpretation seems to take no account of the
strictly religious meaning of ritual in cosmic religion. For the latter presupposes the intervention of
a divine power.

Mircéa Eliade seems to point in the right direction when he relates ritual to myth. Ritual is an
imitation, not of the realities of the physical cosmos, but of the archetypal deeds performed in primordial time as divine actions. Ritual is the setting
in motion of these divine actions. "By no matter
what ritual and, consequently, by no matter what
meaningful act, the primitive enters mythical time,
for the age of myth should not be regarded simply
as a period of the past, but rather as present and
also future, as a state no less than as a period.

This period is creative in the sense that it is then that the creation and organization of the cosmos took place, as well as the revelation of all the archetypal activities. A rite is the repetition of original time."[27]

Here again we cannot but be struck by the resemblance between cosmic and biblical ritual. In these two domains, we see immersion signifying purification, a meal signifying communion with the godhead, sacrifice signifying recognition of divine sovereignty. Not only the acts, but the times and places of the cult are the same in all religions. Easter is first of all the cosmic spring festival; then it becomes the Jewish feast of the exodus from Egypt, and then the Christian feast of the resurrection. Jerusalem was a Canaanite high place before it became the abode of Yahweh and the place of Christ's sacrifice. It is worth noting that the Bible, far from trying to mask it, underlines this continuity.

But if the acts are the same, signifying in this way the unity of the history of salvation, they are charged with new meaning and virtue. Cosmic rites are essentially related to the life of nature. They aim at ensuring the preservation of the cosmos, the regular pattern of rain and harvest, the fruitfulness of families and flocks. The pouring out of water is a sacrament, an effective symbol of fructifying rain; the initiation rite brings man into the tribal community; the spring festival aims at ensuring the renewal of the earth at the beginning of the year; the sacrifice draws down the protection of God on the harvest and wards off evil powers. The cosmic rite is based on the idea that the cosmic order depends on divine power. This is indeed the meaning which it is given in the Bible, where we are taught that the cosmic covenant is the promise which God has made to send rain and fruitful seasons. The object of the rite is to remind God of this promise.

On the other hand, the Christian sacrament, and also the Jewish ritual, are related to the historical acts of God. These interventions are both unique and universal. The event of the flight from Egypt, like that of the resurrection, takes place only once. But the rite at the same time commemorates it and makes it actual in such a way as to focus its efficacy on all times and places. However, the Christian rite has no relation with the cosmic realm. It does not aim at acquiring material benefits, but spiritual benefits. It is an anticipation and a prophecy of eschatological realities to which it already ensures participation. It provides entry into another world, instead of ensuring the preservation of this world. But by retaining the forms of the cosmic liturgy, it reveals that it is truly the same God who first gave natural life and now gives spiritual life.

Cosmic symbolism, myths and rites, have brought before us the collective structure of the non-biblical religions. But side by side with these forms of communal religious life, there is the realm of individual religious experience, the personal relationship of the soul with God. This is a territory on the fringes of cosmic religion, often confused with it. No longer is it a question of ensuring the protection of the godhead for the preservation of nature and the race, but of entering into personal contact with the godhead, beyond nature and the race altogether. Within the scheme that is available to historical enquiry, these aspirations appear in the schools of *nabi* or *bhiksu,* where the practices of asceticism and mysticism are taught. We encounter these in Japanese Buddhism, in Greek Orphism, in Semitic Shamanism.

The most general form of this personal relation with the godhead is *bhakti,* the *eusébeia* of the Greeks, the *pietas* of the Latins. It appears wherever the godhead is conceived not merely as a power from which benefits are sought, and whose anger is feared, but where God becomes an object of love. The religious literature of the pagans provides admirable examples of this type of devotion. The form in which piety is expressed is that of prayer. This is one of the fundamental structures of religion. Prayer takes many forms—praise, acts of grace, supplication. It is the essential activity of personal religion, in that it implies recognition of a godhead with whom the soul can enter into communication and communion, and whose pre-eminent value it accepts.

Piety is evidently common to pagan and biblical religion. But here again it is important to present the problem correctly. The existence of religious instincts is a universal human fact. There are great religious geniuses outside Christendom. But just the same, as we have said, it is not religious feeling that counts, for in itself this does not save. The unique property of the Bible is the revelation of the coming of salvation. From that time forward, the essential activity of religion becomes that of faith. Does this mean, however, that religious feeling is a pagan contamination of Christianity, as many Protestants suppose? Here again we must return to the general law of the relationship between Christian revelation and cosmic religion. By revealing the new birth of faith, biblical religion does not destroy the riches of the religious soul, but rather takes them over. Whereas pagan prayer often goes astray in its search for an object, and incarnates it in an illusory god, Christian piety is directed to the Father of Jesus Christ, to God, the Three in One. But it is the full range of the religious instinct that, once directed towards its true goal, finds there its fulfilment.

However, the supreme goal of individual religion is not piety, but union with the godhead. This is the realm which we call mysticism or spirituality. The soul longs to find her foundation in God beyond the world and beyond herself. This brings us to another form of personal religion, that of *dharma,* the *askesis* of the Greeks. Here it is above all a question not of prayer, but of a disciplined practice, an inward technique. This technique of *dharma* consists of a series of exercises in concentration, which withdraw the soul from the agitation of images and desires, restore her to herself, and give her the power to pass beyond herself into an ecstasy of union with the godhead.

Here is the problem of pagan mysticism and Christian mysticism which we have mentioned. It is undeniable that the methods of purification, the experiences of union described by a Plotinus and by a John of the Cross show striking similarities. But the difference between them is none the less fundamental. The inward experience of the cosmic religions is obtained, as we have said, by appropriate techniques. The Christian mystics also use these techniques. But it remains a fact that for them mystical experience is quite independent of such methods. It is determined, rather, by the action of God in the soul, which is conditioned by nothing whatever.[28] In this respect, even the term "spirituality" is ambiguous. For Eastern mysticism, it means the capture by human consciousness, through the path of decantation, of the spiritual—that is, the immaterial—principle that lies within. But, for the Christian adept, spirituality is that which sets the Holy Spirit in motion within the soul, by an act which is entirely divine.

Thus mysticism does not seem to differ from the other forms of cosmic religion. It is simply the inward development of the cosmic process. Instead of God being known through visible symbols, He is now revealed through His invisible image, which is the human soul. In this sense there is an authentic "natural" mysticism.[29] Mysticism thus appears as a new way by which cosmic religion may know

God; after the cosmic symbol, after the witness of conscience, it arises as the action of the spirit. Such action is a definite image of God, who by this means teaches us something beyond what we have glimpsed in nature. But just as cosmic religion feels after God through hierophanies, and is degraded in idolatry when it sees the sun or a tree as God; so the danger of mysticism is that of divinizing the spirit of man himself, of identifying the *noêton* with the *theion,* as Plotinus and Buddha did, and of thus abandoning the cruder material idols, only to be enslaved by that more subtle idol which is the spirit of man himself.

Christian mysticism will not by any means reject what is authentic in this natural mysticism, any more than it will reject the other forms of cosmic religion; but it will give them a new content. For Christian mysticism, it is not only the natural activity of the spirit that is the mirror in which God the Creator is to be seen, but it is through supernatural acts initiated by the Trinity who dwells within, that the Christian mystic perceives in a mysterious fashion the presence of God. Thus St. Gregory of Nyssa and St. Augustine took over the expressions of Plotinus about the knowledge of God in the mirror of the pure soul, but they gave them an entirely new meaning.[30]

In the foregoing pages we have attempted to place the pagan religions in a biblical perspective from a positive standpoint, by showing the religious values which they contain, and in what respect, nevertheless, they differ fundamentally from the biblical religions. We concluded by seeing in them the sign of a phase in the history of salvation, that of the cosmic covenant, which became outmoded from the time when the covenant with Abraham inaugurated a new development. But this way of putting it is abstract and incomplete. In fact, pagan religions never present cosmic revelation in the pure state, but always more or less deformed. At this stage, indeed, man, as St. Paul says, "feels after God," without the light of positive revelation. The result is that, if it is the true God whom he seeks, the picture which he contrives is always faulty.

We must now point out the chief malformations of the idea of God in these religions. They can be arranged under three headings: polytheism, pantheism, and dualism. Polytheism is the malformation of the primitive religious soul. For her, as we have said, the cosmos is full of hierophanies. The water that leaps from the spring, the storm that bursts forth in thunder and lightning, the moon that illuminates the night, all these are wonders that seem to her to be signs of mysterious forces, which she pictures as beings more powerful and intelligent than herself. Thus the world is peopled with gods. Apollo lets fly the arrows of the sun. Neptune rules the waves of the ocean, Demeter the fruitful harvest; the Naiads bid water leap from the springs, and the Dryads lurk beneath the leaves of the oak-trees.

Greek and Latin literature has made us familiar

with the gods of the Hellenic and Roman world. The days of the week, the months of the year, keep Mars and Venus, Jupiter and Saturn, Janus and Maia, always alive in our memory. But all the pagan religions, including the highest, have their own polytheism. India in particular knows Vishnu, the well-disposed and kindly god, and Siva, the savage god of the Himalayan glaciers; Krishna, the god who mingles in the nightly revels of shepherdesses, and whose praise is celebrated in the Bhagavadgita; Radha, the feminine goddess; Ishvara, the living god of *bhakti*.[31] Through the lofty speculations which develop the theology of India on these themes, their deep-seated connection with the forces of life and vegetation remains as clear as that of the Demeter and Zeus of the Greeks.

Certainly this polytheism is often arranged in a hierarchic manner. The notion of a supreme god appears among the primitive religions of Australia. India perceives, amid her many deities, the manifestation of a single principle. Roman religion of the third century A.D. identifies the supreme god with the sun; secondary gods follow after, and form a celestial pantheon. Then there are the countless *divas,* the *daimones* of the Greeks, hosts of deities that rule over all the functions of life, all the realities of nature, all the happenings of family life, in every quarter of the home. St. Augustine speaks with somewhat heavy irony of these household gods, which he likens to our angels.

But to be precise—and this is what Origen replies to Celsus[32]—the mistake is to take them for gods.

The Christian also believes that mysterious beings rule over fountains and forests, watch over families and cities, protect the young child, and lead souls to Paradise. But he is careful not to make these beings into divinities. They are angels, creatures like men.[33] Catholicism is often accused of having restored paganism and satisfied the spontaneous polytheism of simple people with the cult of the Virgin, the angels and the saints. But it is one thing to be aware of countless protective presences surrounding mankind, and quite another to regard these as divine beings.

Thus the polytheist hierarchy remains within the polytheist orbit. You cannot call yourself a monotheist, just because you have a supreme god. More satisfying to the spirit, this hierarchical paganism is still marred by the basic error of polytheism. How far this error corresponds to the inclination of the religious soul, how far it is normal to people the world with sacred presences, the history of the Hebrews makes abundantly clear. Two thousand years were needed to plant the roots of monotheism deep in a humanity which is only too ready to raise altars to Astarte in sacred woods and on high places. Was not the presence of these neighborly, easy-going, and yet powerful and mysterious gods to be as if physically sensed, when the shadows engulfed the woods and the silence seemed full of their approach?

This is why we understand that there may be in paganism an element which the Fathers of the Church rightly attacked with such violence. Even if the myths and rites were bearers of divine realities, the polytheism with which they were colored would falsify them entirely. And how difficult it was to uproot this element from human souls! It is popular paganism that was the great obstacle to the Gospel. Even the word "pagan" smacks of the elemental religion of the countryside, with all its manifold superstitions. Even we, whom the faith has torn away from false gods—with what difficulty does our imagination avert its gaze from their marvelous stories, which still bewitch us in our dreams!

If polytheism is the error of popular cosmic religion, pantheism is its metaphysical temptation. We may say that this is the point at which disaster has come to all the non-biblical religions, and particularly to the higher ones—equally to the Hinduism of Sankara and to the Neo-Platonism of Plotinus. In fact, reduction to unity is the irresistible inclination of the metaphysical spirit, as also of mystical religiosity. The manifold seems to it a debasement which must be reabsorbed. For this reason the Christian assertion that the Three is as primitive as the One, and that it constitutes the structure of Being, is the greatest of paradoxes. It is the fact that the Trinity exists in God Himself that guarantees the corresponding fact that human persons exist in the Creation.

The characteristic of pantheism is to eliminate the frontiers that separate God from what is not God, to misunderstand at once God's absolute transcendence (since all is in some sense divine) and the existence of the creature (since it does not exist apart from God, but is finally drawn back to Him). Pantheism may assume many forms. For Pythagorism and Platonism (with which Gnosticism is bound up) it appears as the identification of the intelligible with the divine. Every soul is a parcel of divinity, imprisoned in the world of sense and clamoring to be liberated so that it may return to its true homeland. In Plotinus this unity takes the dynamic form of a hierarchy of hypostases which are at the same time a debasement and an unfolding of the One, and which return to Him by a movement of contraction (*epistrophè*).

But the true homeland of pantheism is, geographically speaking, India. Nowhere is the intuition of the essential unity of all so completely expressed as there. Every human soul, *âtman,* is merely a mode of the universal soul, *brahman.* When man enters into himself, he coincides beyond himself with this universal soul, which is more than he can ever be. The philosophy of Sankara brings forward this conception in the form of a fundamental acosmism, for which the world, the cosmos, is a mere illusion, a dream from which one wakes, in which the primordial unity is the only thing that really is. But popular tradition sees in the world of appearances, *maya,* a manifestation of *brahman,* and as it were the outer fringes of its cosmic garment.

In this perspective, God is not really transcendent, since nothing is distinct from Him. He is the fundamental identity beneath apparent multiplicity. This gives us a complementary explanation of the difference between cosmic mysticism and biblical mysticism. For cosmic mysticism, the temptation is pantheism, which makes the soul believe that it is fundamentally divine. Henceforth the mystical struggle is to detach this basis of the soul, which is God Himself, from all that covers and obscures it. But to find God is merely to find the divine in oneself. On the other hand, for biblical mysticism God is utterly inaccessible, separated from man by His fundamental transcendence. All human effort is therefore powerless to grasp Him. He is only possessed when He gives Himself, and He never gives Himself except through love. Thus, by a crucial turning of the tables, it is *agapè,* the movement of love descending from God, which is vital, and not *erôs,* the mounting up of human desire toward Him.

On the other hand, if God does not have an existence of his own apart from man, man does not have an existence of his own apart from God. Being fundamentally identical with Him, it is finally in Him that man is reabsorbed. This brings us to a further difference between cosmic and Christian mysticism. The final result, in the case of the former, is a fusion in which man dissolves in the One. Personality, insofar as it implies distinct existence, is felt to be a limitation. Where God is no longer personal (*Ishvara,* the personal god, is a second hypostasis of the impersonal *Brahman*), man is not a person. Christian mysticism, on the contrary, is a union of love which presupposes a distinction of persons. It is creative love on the part of God, making man subsist before Him as an object of love. It is the return of love to man, who relates himself freely to the God from whom he has received his own being.

All this leads us to the absence in cosmic religions of any clear idea of Creation, insofar as this idea implies a fundamental distinction between God and the creature, the distinct existence of the creature with relation to God, and the unending permanence of the creature. For pantheism, on the contrary, according to Valéry, "the universe is only a fault in the purity of Non-Being," of totally indeterminate Being. The cosmogonies of the cosmic religions are not recitals of creation, but the unfolding of the diversity of nature on the part of a primordial germ, a cosmic egg or *tohuv'bohu.* It is interesting to note that the first chapter of *Genesis,* taking up the material elements of the Chaldaean and Canaanite cosmogonies, fundamentally modifies their meaning, by introducing into them the idea of creation, *bara,* that is, an integrally divine act which arouses existence out of nothingness and not simply the unfolding of eternally existent being.

The final pantheism of mysticism thus corresponds to the initial pantheism of mythology. It is the movement of contraction that corresponds to that of expansion. In this respect there is no basic difference between the conception of God held by the primitive cosmogonies and those of the most highly evolved pagan mysticisms. We find in each the same hovering of thought, the same hesitation on the frontiers of divinity, the same dissipation amid intermediary stages. Only biblical revelation will bear the sharp sword of God's Word into this darkness, and implacably descry the sphere of the divine and the sphere of the created. Nowhere is more clearly seen than here the difficulty of the human spirit left to its own devices in its quest for God, struggling to work out a worthwhile idea of Him.

It remains to be said that pantheism is the perversion and the clumsy misinterpretation of a sound intuition. Just as polytheism is the malformation of piety, of *bhakti,* in search of the object of its adoration, and multiplied to the *n*th degree, so pantheism is the malformation of the reality of the divine immanence. For if God is beyond everything, He is also in everything. It is also true that He is present in the cosmos which is His temple. St Paul made this clear to the pagans of Athens: "For in him we live, and move, and are."[34] It is still more true that He is present in the soul and "not far from every one of us."[35] But this divine presence is a closed book to pantheism, which fails to recognize it in the reality of a personal God "who is all that is and nothing that is."

The third perversion of the cosmic religions is dualism. Although we can find elements of this in many of the pagan religions, it only appears as a major element in some of them. It characterizes the Iranian Mazdaism of Zoraster, who opposes the light-principle, Ahura-Mazda, to the dark-principle, Ahriman. But above all it takes on a vast development and becomes a world religion in Gnosticism, which appeared at roughly the same time as Christianity, and under the name of Manichaeism spread into North Africa and Chinese Turkestan

from the fourth to the seventh centuries.[36] It still
has a real attraction for the modern mind. Simone
Weil, for example, found Gnosticism more congenial
to her spirit than any other religion.

We must be clear about the nature of dualism.
It is not a matter of maintaining the existence of
two gods, equal and opposite. As Simone Pètrement
has well shown, dualists are monotheists. They do
not call God the principle of evil, but they believe
"that the world contains a principle completely alien to good, a substance which never took its rise
from God, and which is, if not evil, at least the
cause of evil."[37] We see, then, the problem that
dualism is concerned with—the problem of the existence of evil. It is a fact that evil exists; yet its
existence could not be attributed to God. How can
its existence be explained? Neo-Platonism and Hinduism regard it as an illusion. Knowledge will cause
it to disappear. But this solution is hard put to
explain its ever having arisen. Christianity sees here
the effect of the liberty of angels and men created
good but, being distinct from God, not being good
by essence; consequently a fault is able to creep in
between being and good, and that fault is the
power of evil. Evil is a result of contingency, that
is, of creation. It can only arise where there is a
creature distinct from God. It is in this context that
the idea of creation appears once again as the cor-
nerstone of biblical revelation.

The dualist solution is different. Evil is a reality
which has its own existence and owes nothing to
God or man. It is part of being; it is a principle

sui generis. This principle seems generally to be identified by the Gnostics with matter, which is not created by God and is a principle distinct from Him. The Gnosticism of Valentinus sees in the cosmos the work of a Demiurge, who is a kind of clumsy god, the author of a misshapen plan. It is this Demiurge that he imagines he has found in the God of the Old Testament. Man is born, then, in a badly constructed world. But there is in him nevertheless a spark fallen from the pleroma. The object of Gnosis is to reveal it and so to enable it to get out of the world, to escape from the tyranny of the *cosmokrators,* the planetary demons, to be reunited with the real creation, the luminous world of the aeons, which is the workmanship of the true God.

Dualism is not a primitive religion. It appears in a world where the optimism of cosmic religion has run foul of the reality of evil. It is the counterpart of cosmic religion. All the sacred things that adorned the cosmic Temple are no more than the sordid utensils of the cosmic Prison. The household gods of polytheism become ferocious demons. Dualism is the expression of a guilty conscience, and it brings with it the hope of salvation. That is what gives it such a profoundly human resonance. It is the simplest and clearest reply to the mystery of evil. The work of Puech has shown that it represented one of the basic structures in terms of which the relationship of the world to God was thought out.

Biblical religion retains the truth of Manichaeism.

It declares that evil is not a problem that man can solve for himself, but a mystery which goes beyond him. It shows man as the prisoner of "the Prince of this world," and only to be freed by Christ. But it refuses to see in evil a positive principle endowed with its own existence without nevertheless reducing it to a simple disorder of the human will. It recognizes a mystery of evil, a venomous source from which it leaks out into mankind. But this mystery of evil enters too into the creation of God. It has its origin in a created liberty. It is the mystery of the fall of Lucifer, the angel created good and ruined by his own splendor. It is false, then, to speak, as Simone Pètrement does, of dualism in the Bible or St. Paul. We can only say that there are sometimes dualist infiltrations into Judaism, particularly in the doctrine of the Essenes, such as we find in the *Manual of Discipline,* showing God establishing in the beginning an Angel of darkness in opposition to an Angel of light.

Dualism seems therefore to be a sign of the failure of thought as it strives to picture the relationship between God and the cosmos, just as pantheism is. It is a simpler solution than that of the Bible, but it represents an inability to maintain the fundamental relationship between God and the world, and the fact of the existence of evil. But evil appears to it to be precisely one of those "limit-problems" that reason cannot grasp, and that compel the human mind to remain open to a revelation which can alone initiate it into the final secrets of existence and history.

Thus we have followed the adventures of the pagan religious soul, groping in its own darkness to find that living God who is so near at hand and yet so far away. These adventures provide solid and most valuable evidence of God's truth. We must recognize in such cultic, doctrinal and mystical skirmishings the expression of a revelation of God that speaks to every human soul through the cosmos, the conscience, and the spirit. But, in its quest for God, the pagan soul falls by the wayside. Lacking the support of a positive revelation, it expresses clumsily what it sees; it falters and is deceived. This is the twofold aspect which makes its history a glorious and a deceptive thing, and explains its profound appeal as it rises from the depths of religious manhood towards that light which it will only find in the fullness of Jesus Christ.

BIBLIOGRAPHY

R. Otto, *The Idea of the Holy,* 1950.

Mircéa Eliade, *Traité d'histoire des religions,* 1946.

Georges van der Leeuw, *La Religion dans son essence et ses manifestations,* 1948.

Jean Daniélou, *Les Saints païens de l'Ancien Testament,* 1955.

2

THE GOD OF
the philosophers

The God of the philosophers is one of the signs of the contradictory nature of religious thought. Christian theology, from St. Thomas Aquinas to the Vatican Council, has always maintained the possibility of a rational knowledge of the existence and attributes of God; and this remains a principle of Catholic thinking. But even in the heart of Christianity another current has never ceased to pulsate— that which regards the God of reason as a stumbling-block, to whom the God of faith is opposed. Thus Pascal speaks of "the God of Abraham, Isaac and Jacob, not the God of the philosophers and scholars"; thus Kierkegaard, for whom reason leads to despair, and despair to faith; thus Chestov, contrasting Job, the Christian philosopher, with Socrates, the wise man after the flesh; thus Barth, denouncing the God of the philosophers, in whom the spirit of man is reflected, as the supreme idol.

My plan here is not to inquire whether in the order of existence philosophy has ever led man to God, for this is a fictitious problem. Conversion to God is always a development of the whole man; and since the order in which we find ourselves his-

torically is an order of grace and sin, the real progress of man is not a progress of pure reason. My
purpose here is different. I set myself within this
real order, which is in fact an order of grace,
within the history of salvation. I ask myself what
is the status of philosophy within a theological
perspective, just as I have asked this question about
religion. And as with the God of the religions, I shall
attempt to prove that there is a good and bad use
of philosophy, that there is a false God of the
philosophers, and yet also a true philosophy of God.

Before studying the means by which philosophy
may approach the knowledge of God, we must
first deal with the legitimacy of such a practice,
for this is what is now in question. Its legitimacy
is challenged from widely differing motives. For
some, reason, being fundamentally corrupted on account of original sin, is incapable of attaining to
truth. For others, God being in essence beyond the
capture of the human mind, all claim on the part
of this mind to know Him cannot be other than
illusory. Some are struck by the contradictions among
the philosophers, and think that it is dangerous on
this account to put their faith in God on rational
grounds. Positivist minds, trained in scientific disci-
plines, are disconcerted by the trend of metaphysics,
in which they fail to find their criteria of certainty
and take refuge in religious experience.

All these objections contain something valuable,
and rightly warn us against any blind confidence
in reason. The encyclical *Humani Generis,* while

endorsing the possibility that reason may arrive at the knowledge of God, recognizes that man in fact attains it with difficulty unless he has the support of grace. Moreover, it is true that the ancient philosophers never reached any but imperfect and conflicting notions of God, and that reason has not been able to gain right knowledge of Him except with the help of revelation. This is the meaning that Gilson rightly gives to the idea of Christian philosophy. It is still more true that the living God cannot be circumscribed by the intellect, and that a God who was entirely intelligible to man would surely not be the true God. Finally it is true that metaphysical certainties belong to another order than mathematical certainties, and that the same criteria of evidence cannot be applied to both.

But all the same, do the limitations of reason justify us in depreciating it? Many men of our time contrast it with personal religious experience. Certainly it is a fact that the knowledge of the true God always implies a personal encounter and an inward conversion. But first of all, religious experience is pre-eminently subjective. The certainty to which it attains is incommunicable. One is tempted to conclude, then, that the knowledge of God is the expression of an instinct connected with man's psychological structure. There will be religious and nonreligious temperaments; belief in God will be regarded as the expression of an inner need, the projection of a thirst for happiness which cannot be satisfied by any created thing.

There is no need to emphasize the danger of such

an outlook. It justifies the frequent taunt of non-believers who hold that belief in God is prompted by the need for security, inward comfort and consolation. To this we must reply that belief in God has nothing to do with the religious instinct. It is objectively imposed alike on the mystical and the positive temperament. But far from admitting that the harmony between God's existence and our affective desires is a criterion of His existence, we must state on the contrary that God's reality is imposed on us far more in an objective manner, in that He contradicts our desires, in that His reality disconcerts our intellect and His will upsets our plans, in that we are compelled to recognize Him, in some sense against our will.

On the other hand, if it is true that the encounter with God is a personal event, it is no less true that this event needs afterwards to be controlled and placed within the scheme of things. It is never a development of pure reason, but it must always be subsequently submitted to criticism and sifted by reason. It is only then that I can make certain that I am not the plaything of an illusion, that I am not being carried away by an affective impulse. Only a belief in God which has thus been tested by reason and found solid, which has been brought into relation with the other data and acknowledged to be consistent with them, carries real weight and assures us that our conviction has a sound basis.

Just as reason is necessary to the establishment of the knowledge of God, so is it necessary in exercising this knowledge. Nothing is more dangerous than a religion that claims to have outdistanced reason; it can only lead to fanaticism, illuminism, obscurantism; it is lost in a jungle of superstition. Above all, it runs the risk of being an idle solution. Recourse to the supernatural easily turns into an escapist's paradise. It claims to find mystery where there may only be ignorance, and thus to justify the positivist critic for whom religion corresponds to a prescientific stage of thought. But the true religious mystery is quite different; it is concerned with what cannot be explained in any other way. Yet there is a danger of confusing the two regions. The function of scientific criticism is precisely that of clearing up this confusion.[1]

If rationalism, and that pride of the mind which claims to possess God and deal with Him, are a serious danger, how noble, on the other hand, are the courageous efforts of the intellect which in respect for mystery never renounces its determination to understand, which goes on to the limit of its capacity and never halts until it is conquered by the overwhelming pressure of a blinding light! This boldness of the intellect in exploring the mystery is the quality on which the imperishable greatness of St. Thomas Aquinas rests. It implies a difficult equilibrium, seldom realized, between the abyss of rationalism and that of fideism. But it is doubtless this perfectly balanced equilibrium which the instinct of the Church acknowledged when she proclaimed him as the supreme theologian.

This is particularly relevant to the very problem

we are discussing. For none has shown better than he, both the limitations and the value of the rational knowledge of God. First, as to the limitations: until his time Christian philosophers, especially St. Augustine, more or less yielded to the temptation presented by Platonism, of seeing in the divine the proper object of the intellect, obscured only by its immersion in the flesh. St. Thomas had the courage to break entirely with this tendency, and to refuse to admit there we could form for ourselves any sound or intelligible notion of God, since our concepts are always abstracted from the sensible world. He thus reaffirmed the view of Gregory of Nyssa whom, however, he scarcely knew. Christian tradition gave him good reason to reject any kind of ontologism, and to deny that there could be any natural intuition of God.

Thus reason can never approach God except mediately, insofar as His existence is postulated by the contingency of what it does not attain. Reason can affirm existence and transcendence. But, as Gilson says so well in his summary of St. Thomas' thought: "Once this is said, all that man can say is said. This divine essence, whose existence he assumes, is not penetrated by his intellect, and we know that of himself he will never reach it. Denys is right in saying that the God towards whom our reason strives is still, so to speak, an unknown God. For we know well that He is, and what He is not. But what He is remains for us entirely unknown." [2] In other words, reason can know God—and that is her supreme greatness; but she can know Him only from outside, and that is her infinite limitation. Reason is compelled to affirm Him in order to remain faithful to herself; and by this very affirmation reason recognizes her limits.

But this is at the same time a courageous affirmation of the power of reason. For if the knowledge that she has of God is never adequate, it is none the less perfectly real. There is no trace in St. Thomas of skepticism or agnosticism. In fact, reason has a secure knowledge of God's existence. The latter, as necessary cause, is implied in the existence of contingent being; as absolute truth, it is presupposed by the very exercise of the intellect; as perfect good, it is postulated by the existence of morality. Not only does reason know His existence, but she can form for herself some idea of Him, insofar as He participates in contingent being, and insofar as all the perfections of the latter are a defective, but real, image of His infinite perfection.

We must go further still. Imperfect as it is, the created spirit still has a capacity to become all things. If its proper object is created being, it remains true that no created being exhausts its possibilities. It is thus a frontier between two worlds, as St. Thomas admirably describes it. The created spirit lies on the far side of all determinate beings, and yet remains on the near side of that Being who transcends all determinacy. Thus, if it cannot directly grasp Him, there is yet in it an instinct to grasp Him, the "natural desire" of that real, though ineffective, vision which the grace of God could bring to perfection by communicating to it, through grace, a mysterious share in the divine Being.[3]

Such is the admirable manner in which St. Thomas defines the status of reason in the sphere of the knowledge of God. By presenting at the same time in a rigorous fashion the value and the limitations of the rational knowledge of God, he reveals the paradox of the philosophical quest. For God is at the same time its object and its boundary, its supreme end and its question-mark. The goal of philosophy is to prove His existence, but she can only do this by acknowledging her powerlessness. In that she refuses to make this confession of her limitations, in that she yields to the Platonist temptation, the God whom she arrives at is not the true God. In fact, it is clear that, as Gregory of Nyssa says, "God being beyond all determinacy, he who thinks that God is something determinate deceives himself when he believes that what he knows is God." [4] Thus the problem of God reveals the inward contradiction of philosophy; and it is here that at the same time He justifies her and defines her position.

But it is precisely this position, which constitutes the status of philosophy in the Christian scheme of things, that the majority of philosophers refuse to accept. Philosophy seems to them to lose its significance if it lacks a complete grasp of the intelligibility of being, if it is not supreme knowledge. They do not resign themselves to having to acknowledge a principle which is not perfectly intelligible to them. It is this perfect intelligibility that they call by the name of God; and it is this false

God of the philosophers that we may justly oppose to the God of Abraham, Isaac and Jacob. But this deity is not the God of reason, but the idol of rationalism.

Let us be more precise. The requirement of philosophy is a requirement of intelligibility. Confronted by the apparent disorder of things, the philosophical mind seeks to establish order, to build up sequences, to demonstrate a chain of causes. Beyond concrete realities, it seeks to disclose the very structure of being itself. In this search for being, it desires to arrive at the first principle, that which is at once the cause, the pattern, the end of all that is. This principle is called God. The philosophical quest comes necessarily to the problem of God, which is in reality the only one that concerns it.

But here it meets temptation. For the principle which it calls God, it arrives at through its demand for intelligibility. He represents for philosophy a requirement. Philosophy proceeds to apply to God the principle which has led it to Him; God is expected also to be intelligible, and the intelligibility that philosophy applies to Him is the law of the human mind. Thus philosophy proceeds to define Him with its accustomed categories, calling Him the One, intellectual Love, absolute Mind, and so forth. Many great philosophers have reduced the totality of the real to a perfectly coherent system, of which God is the immanent law. Their mind is perfectly satisfied with thus having mastered the totality of being.

But it happens that, by a strange contradiction,

it is precisely at the moment when they imagine in their audacity that they have reached God that they have in reality lost Him. In fact, they thought they had reached Him when the demand of their mind for intelligibility was completely satisfied. But for all that, they had made their mind the measure of God. Yet the very essence of God is precisely to be that which is measured by nothing and which measures all things. On the level of God, the problem of intelligibility is reversed. He is the unintelligible for whom everything else is intelligible. But in reducing Him to intelligibles, they deny His specific reality. He is not found within intelligibility, but He is that which constitutes it. So, as Pascal says, the most reasonable course is the disavowal of reason; and that is where the knowledge of God lies.

But this runs counter to the claims of reason. She refuses to leave open this wound in her side, this crack in her edifice. Erecting into an absolute the intelligibility which is proper to herself, she pulls everything down to that level. She cannot allow anything to escape her. She refuses to acknowledge that she is checkmated; yet it is just this checkmate that was the knowledge of God which threw wide the gates of mystery. She would have found God by acknowledging her powerlessness; she loses Him by claiming to possess Him. The One of Plotinus, the Brahman of Sankara, the Being of Spinoza, the absolute Mind of Hegel, are finally idols, not so much by being the object of reason as by being the sufficiency of reason.

The error of all rationalism is that of putting

God on the same basis as other objects of reason, higher, no doubt, but not really other. To paraphrase Gabriel Marcel, God cannot be treated as a problem. He represents the boundary of reason. His dazzling light prevents the eye from seeing Him. Consequently, all that we say of Him is inadequate. He cannot be contained by any concept. But at the same time all that we say of Him is true. "He is all that is and nothing that is," says Pseudo-Dionysus. The moderns will say knowledge of Him is dialectical, *i.e.* that all statements about Him imply their opposite. Already St. Thomas showed that all that is said of Him must also be denied, that negative theology is the necessary complement of positive theology. This is that very doctrine of analogy which enables us to speak of God in words borrowed from creation, but on condition that we make it clear that they apply to Him in a different way from that in which they apply to His creatures.

Moreover, we can see that what is true of God is also true of other "limit-problems" which imply an apparent contradiction, and about which it is only possible to construct propositions that seem to be irreconcilable because the place where they are reconciled is beyond the reach of sight. So with liberty, which is a limit-problem, and one that is irreducible to complete intelligibility, since we must at the same time say that man is free and that God is the cause of all and since nobody has ever shown or will ever show how these two statements are to be reconciled. So, too, with evil, which is imposed upon us as a tragic reality, and seems irreconcilable with the goodness of God. The real problems of metaphysics are also those that bring metaphysics up against a boundary line.

But their function is precisely to do this. They prevent reason from getting shut in on herself, they are windows opening toward the mystery of being. That mystery cannot be fathomed by reason, but at least she can lead towards it, and this is indeed her function. She leads the spirit as far as her frontiers, she discerns the region of mystery. By clarifying all that is within her domain, she prevents us from placing the mystery where it does not lie. She de-mystifies the natural realities that people are trying to make into mysteries. This is her critical, purifying function. But none the less she points towards the true mysteries. She would betray her mission if she refused to acknowledge them and denied the reality of all that the brightness of her gaze does not penetrate.

But these limit-problems, the thresholds of reason, are not only characterized by the fact that they are placed somewhat beyond her reach and so cannot be neatly defined. Another feature that they possess is that they cannot be broached from the standpoint of straightforward discussion, but demand a total outlook, an existential conversion. So it is with suffering—all attempts to provide an explanation are unbearable. We cannot hold a discussion with a man who is suffering. That is what Job's comforters did and it cannot be tolerated. Neither can suffering be analyzed and counter-attacked. This is why Christ seems the only answer to it, because He gives no rational explanation, but unravels it existentially.[5] So, too, with hell, which is a limit-problem, at the same time <u>necessary</u> (for without it nothing would any longer be important or serious) and nevertheless intolerable—and again it can only be met by an existential attitude.

If limit-problems compel us to conversion, that is because they involve the being of a person, they engage his existence. I have no right to treat anyone as a mere object of thought; moreover it is impossible to do so, for a person represents a nucleus irreducible by discursive analysis; he presents himself as existing in himself, as a distinct spiritual center. This irreducible nucleus can only be reached by love, which compels me to go out of myself. This is why an idealist philosophy that reduces everything to thought is a truncated philosophy. An integral philosophy could only be a spiritual realism, which would compel me to hold on by love to the person of the other, and make me reach in that other what is really real, *i.e.* what I cannot make use of, what cannot be reduced to having and remains in the region of being.

This is really true of God. He is, above all, the one whom I cannot make use of. The error of false philosophies is precisely that of making God an object, of claiming to possess Him through the intellect. But that which the intellect possesses could not be God. On the contrary, it must be said that the encounter with God drives the intellect to a fundamental conversion, to a decentralization from the self; and this conversion is the knowledge of God Himself. For God can only be broached as an existent and as a personal existent. On His level, my act of intellect seems itself to be an existential act, the act of an existent; and thus far it depends on God. To know God is not, then, to hold Him in my intellect, but on the contrary to rediscover myself as measured by Him.

So we see at the same time how the knowledge of God is a work of reason and a challenge to reason. It is in this sense that "nothing is more reasonable than the disavowal of reason." Reason is the necessary means of knowledge in that she prevents us from placing God where He is not, and keeps us from idols, including that of the mind of man himself. Surveying the world of bodies and the world of spirits, she fails to find God there. She implores the angels to reveal His name, but they refuse to tell it. Then "she understands that the true knowledge of Him whom she seeks and her true vision consist in seeing that He is invisible and in knowing that He transcends all knowledge, separated from all things by His incomprehensibility as by darkness." [6]

We have tried to make clear the status of the philosophical knowledge of God within the Christian scheme, and we arrive at a twofold result: reason can know God's existence when she operates in the region which alone is real, *i.e.* that of existent being, and when, leaving contingent existence behind, she links it again to God as a personal existent.

This implies an existential relationship between reason and perception; by reflecting on herself as an existent subject, reason comes to acknowledge her relationship to an existent transcendent subject who is God.

But for all that, she does not grasp who this God is. He is the object of a statement, not of an intuition. His existence is stated, but His *ousia* remains unknowable—and that precisely is the heart of the matter. For reason, to know God is to state the existence of the unknowable, *i.e.* the existence of that which transcends her knowledge; and it is clear that the claim to know "what" this unknowable "is" would be the denial of its essence. This would put it in the world of that which is on the level of reason, and it would then be no longer a question of God. That is the core of the paradox of the knowledge of God, that is what makes it an order apart, on the frontiers of knowledge and non-knowledge.

But we must establish that the concourse of philosophies has proved its inability to remain on this narrow frontier, and that they almost always run to one excess or another. Exaggerating the non-knowledge of God, they will arrive either at agnosticism, which refuses to say anything about Him, even that He exists, and maintains a questioning position, or at atheism, which denies the existence of that which lies beyond the light of reason. Or, exaggerating knowledge, they will claim to possess God's essence; but the God whom they think they know is only their own mind, so they run either into rationalism, which reduces God to the measure of the intelligible realities of the mind, or into pantheism, which makes Him the immanent inward being of all reality, the primordial unity of all things. In each of these ways they fail to reach Him as a person, therefore it is not Him whom they reach.

Must we, then, resign ourselves to saying nothing about God without making an attempt to define His transcendence? At first sight, yes. To affirm God is surely in effect to affirm that He is nothing that falls within the field of our experience, that He is altogether Other; and it remains true that this is the first thing we must say about Him. The great patristic theologians rightly insisted on this incomprehensibility of the divine essence, against the Christian Neo-Platonist Eunonius, who declared that the notion of unbegotten, *agennêtos,* was an adequate concept of the divine essence. Against him, John Chrysostom, Gregory of Nyssa, Cyril of Jerusalem, were never weary of affirming that the divine *ousia* was a mystery inaccessible to human reason.

But in face of this, it is true also that, if we cannot directly know, by an immediate intuition, the divine nature, something of it is accessible to our intellect through the created world. We have already seen, in relation to cosmic religion, that visible realities are hierophanies of God, and that the human soul is His created image. This is true of all the realities of this world. Thus each of them tells us something about God. Having said that we can say nothing about Him, we must now say that we can say an infinite number of things about Him. We find here once again the paradox which is always presented by the knowledge of God. We must at the same time deny everything about Him and affirm everything about Him. It is this union of positive and negative theology that gives us the true knowledge of God.

No writer has shown this better than Pseudo-Dionysus. "Thus instructed," he says, "the theologians unite in praising God for having no name and for possessing all names. For having no name, since they report that the Thearchy herself, in one of the mystical visions in which she revealed herself symbolically, reproved him who asked her: What is your name? and to turn him away from all knowledge that can be expressed by a name, spoke thus: Why ask me my name? It is excellent —and for having many names, when they afterwards describe her as saying of herself: I Am That I Am, or again Life, Light, God, Truth. Afterwards they say that this divine principle belongs to intellects, to souls and bodies, that it is identical harmony in the bosom of the identical, in the universe, around the universe, beyond the Universe, Superessential, Sun, Star, Fire, Water, Spirit, Dew, Cloud, Absolute Rock, Stone, in a word, all that is and nothing that is." [7]

So we can understand the remark of that old Christian who said to Origen: "It is always dangerous to speak of God." For every time I say something about Him, I must immediately say the opposite. In fact, there is a great danger of pic-

turing God in the image of man. This anthropomorphic representation of God arouses difficulties in
many minds. They rightly reject a representation of
God which seems to them to bring Him down to
human realities. But if I say nothing of God, I
thus betray my mission as a theologian. To speak
of Him I must use words borrowed from human experience and proclaim His love or His beauty, while
knowing how much these expressions lend themselves
to equivocation. Such is the tragic position of the
theologian, who must speak of what is beyond
speech. Such, too, is the difficulty of using analogies.
I shall only give one example of this, but it is a
crucial one—the possibility, for reason, of knowing
that God is personal. I mean by this that He
possesses pre-eminently the perfection which personality on the human level constitutes. Even the
idea of impersonal mind is a contradiction. The person seems to be the supreme value on the human
level, and therefore it must needs exist in God.

This, then, is an essential truth; one is all the
more struck by the fact that most philosophers
have overlooked or misunderstood it. The Ancients
seem hardly to have reached it. This is certainly
true of Indian philosophy, which has never been
able to bear the idea of divine transcendence; and
if Plato or Plotinus glimpsed something of divine
personality, they never expressed it clearly. It is
after the Revelation that philosophy was able to
make this ultimate progress in the natural knowledge that it could have of God. "Theoretically,"
writes Borne with justice, "reason could have risen

by her own efforts to the notion of a personal God; but in fact it was necessary for her attention to be attracted by faith towards charity, in order that she might concern herself with what she already knew implicitly, that God is a person." [8]

Modern philosophers in their turn have stumbled against this idea. The pantheism of Spinoza, as well as the idealism of Hegel or Brunchvicg, deny the impersonality of a God subsisting apart from the world. All their difficulties derive from that of reconciling the infinity of the divine perfection with the limitation that seems to be implied by the notion of personality. "God the person and God the principle of unity exclude one another by all their characteristics," says Parodi, "the former implying determinacy and singularity, the latter infinity and indeterminacy." [9] He could not have expressed more neatly the antinomy which was already a stumbling-block to Plotinus. It results in the rejection of a personal God as an anthropomorphism; God is taken to be nothing but the supreme ideal principle of explanation.

How are we to reply to this difficulty? Some thinkers, struck by the apparent impossibility for philosophy of reconciling these two notions of God, and not wishing to sacrifice either, have admitted that of herself philosophy could only reach God the supreme principle of intelligibility, and that the notion of God the person belonged to the realm of moral and religious experience. Thus Père Laberthonnière contrasted the God of Nature, the unmoved abode of the ideas, of Greek idealism, with

God the Person, the source of life, of Christian realism. Le Roy makes the same distinction: "There is a duality, almost an antinomy, in the prevailing conception of God; for He is regarded from a twofold standpoint—that of metaphysics, in which He appears as the supreme principle of explanation and the center of intelligible unity; and that of morality and religion, in which God is, above all, the basis and guarantee of human values, with whom man enters into spiritual communion. I have maintained that here, in a certain sense, is to be found the contrast between Hellenism and Judaism." [10]

But it seems to us that such a distinction is unacceptable, founded as it is upon the idealist conception of philosophy, which eliminates from the field of metaphysics any consideration of existences, in order to concentrate on intelligibility, on the essence of things. It is abundantly clear that such a philosophy could not admit the idea of a person, which is a perfection of the existential concrete order. But that is an undue mutilation of metaphysics, whose aim is to know beings in all that they require for existence, *i.e.* at the same time in their nature and in their substance. The distinction between God the Person and the God of Nature leads finally to a distinction between two modes of attribution of the divine perfections, those indeed which St. Thomas distinguishes at the beginning of the *Summa*: "*De Deo loquentes utimur nominibus concretis ut significemus ejus subsistenciam, quia apud nos non subsistunt nisi composita, et utimur nomini-*

bus abstractis, ut significemus ejus simplicitatem." [11]
Subsistencia, simplicitas, personality, unity—these
are the very terms of the antinomy presented above
by Parodi, and it is here that we see them resolved.

In opposition to M. Le Roy, who declares that
"pure philosophy is not required to demonstrate any
reality with regard to divine personality," [12] we hold
with Maritain that "metaphysics knows demonstra-
bly that the divine essence subsists in itself as infinite personality." [13] If in fact human reason did
not already know divine personality before the Revelation, she could nevertheless arrive at it by her
own resources, she already knew it implicitly. In
this matter, as in others, Revelation led metaphysics
to the discovery of truths that were new, but that
none the less were strictly metaphysical.

To understand this, we must first of all make it
clear in a general way what are the constituents
of this perfection of personality which we claim to
attribute to God. In fact it is in the very idea
which they have of "person" that for many people the real difficulty lies, when it is a question of
giving this name to God. "Person" is conceived by
them in an anthropomorphic manner, as something
essentially finite; how, on that basis, are they to
avoid contradicting the divine infinity? For if, in
spite of everything, God is to be regarded as a
person, they would have, with Renouvier, to make
Him a finite being. Le Roy puts the antinomy as
follows: "Either we shall define the word 'personality' and so fall into the pit of anthropomor-

phism, or we shall leave it undefined and fall into the no less terrible pit of agnosticism." [14]

I shall not insist on the error that lurks in identifying all "determinacy" (as Parodi did just now) or all "definition" (as Le Roy now does) with limitation. I shall turn without delay to the fundamental charge of anthropomorphism. What do I mean by this? If it is maintained that we ought not to picture God as a human person, with all the imperfections that personality implies in man, I shall be quite willing to agree. "But," as Maritain rightly says, "all that is laborious and complicated, all that is twisted round an inadequate center and based on an inadequate design, in the current usage of the word 'personality,' the whole anthropomorphic burden that weighs the word down, refers uniquely to that in us which connects personality with individuality, and thus with material conditions . . . We must deliver the idea of personality from this matrix, in order to grasp its transcendent value and its anoetic power." [15]

If, on the other hand, by the charge of anthropomorphism we mean a refusal to the mind of the strict right to form positive notions of infinite Being—starting with man, who is a finite being—when these notions do not imply any limitation, the criticism falls to the ground. In fact, between anthropomorphism, strictly understood, and agnosticism, there is a certain analogy. But, rightly considered, the main difficulty that the moderns find in comprehending divine personality is the intellectual contempt which makes them misunderstand the analogy and reject as anthropomorphic every effort aimed at knowing God through the medium of man. This is what Père de Grandmaison replied to M. Le Roy: "Divine personality presents a difficulty if, as it seems, anthropomorphism is here inevitable, and if, in the desire to eliminate it, we risk depriving what we are saying of all precise meaning. It is true that we naturally model our distinct concept of a person on the ever-present reality that we are. But a more careful reflection reveals, beneath this anthropomorphic image which usually conceals them, certain features that do not necessarily imply the mode of human existence, and which surpass human limitations." [16]

We have, therefore, the right to form our own idea of divine personality, beginning with the only personality we know, human personality, but on condition that we only retain its essential features, those that have analogical value and so justify the attribution of personality at once to God and the creature.

Thus we can set aside the preliminary objection that sees in its attribution to God a form of anthropomorphism. We must say, on the other hand, that if, in the order of knowledge, it is on the basis of knowledge of human persons that we form our notion of divine personality, in the order of being it is to God that primarily and properly belongs the personality in which our inadequate human persons are only feeble participations. In fact, there is nothing in the concept of a person that indicates anything other than the perfection of being which is *in itself* at all the levels of knowledge that it implies.

Having said this, it remains for us to ask how the human mind can, by the sole light of intellect, rise to the knowledge of divine personality. The latter results from the absolute independence of God within being, from His aseity. In fact this being which necessarily exists, since it is necessary that there should be being which exists through itself, from the mere fact that it possesses existence in itself, is also necessarily a substance, because that is the very definition of substantial being. It is even the most perfect of substances—since the independence in being which defines substance is not complete in created substances (which are always at the same time dependent), it could only be from Being that they receive existence; while in Being, which is *a se,* there is, on the contrary, absolute sufficiency within itself to exist, a total independence within being. It could not be *a se* without being, by the same token, *in se.* Every form of pantheism is hence excluded. The proper existence of the Creator is irreducibly distinguished from that which He communicates to His creature. Being subsists by essence in itself. *"Ecce distinctio personalis: Ego sum qui sum."* [17] God can say "I."

We may notice, on the other hand, that the transcendence of a personal God is that of a spiritual and willing substance, *i.e.* one that not only subsists in itself, but moreover perfectly possesses itself through the will, and perfectly knows itself through the intellect; it is the transcendence of a being who can say "I." It follows, as we have said, that the divine personality participates, to a sovereign degree, in the "dignity" which attaches to the person as such, and which seems the first thing that comes to mind in the current use of the word; a person is contrasted with a thing in that it has a right to a certain respect. Père de Grandmaison emphasizes this aspect when he defines the person as ". . . a living, knowing, willing and loving *ego* whom one cannot, without doing him an injustice, treat as a thing, who cannot without revaluation be considered as such." [18]

If human personality implies this dignity, it is abundantly clear that, insofar as God has not been conceded personality, there is at least one sense, that of spiritual substance, in which man is not transcended. If God is not a person and man is one, insofar as he is a person, insofar as he judges and chooses, he escapes from the domain of God. Perhaps it would be necessary to seek here for the deep reason which causes the wise men of this world to be reluctant to acknowledge God as a person. In fact it is for this reason that God deserves, to an infinite degree, that respect which we owe to a person as such—and which, in His case, is adoration. It is for this reason that we fundamentally depend on Him, not only in the physical, but in the moral order as well. It is this—that it offends a person and violates the sacred rights of an infinite person—that underlies the gravity of moral evil and marks it off from physical evil. "Because man is a sovereign personality, the notion of sin has meaning: to wound the order of that which is committed to the free-will of self-rule, is to wound God Himself." [19] This also makes it clear, as Gilson remarks,[20] that the true idea of moral good and evil only appeared with the clear idea of a personal God.

Divine personality expresses, above all, the infinite abyss that separates God from His creature. God is sufficient to Himself, the whole Creation lies before Him as pure nothingness, it adds nothing to what He already is. But to this first aspect there is added a second, which seems at first sight to contradict it: the very attribute that succeeds in making God inaccessible is at the same time the one that will permit us to enter into a relationship with Him. "This sovereign personality," says Maritain, "is at once that which removes Him farthest from us—the inflexible infinite stands face to face with me, a wretched mortal—and at the same time brings Him nearest to us, since the incomprehensible purity has a countenance, a voice, and has set me before it so that I may gaze upon Him, so that I may speak to Him and He to me." [21]

A new aspect now appears in the notion of personality. After incommunicability, communicativeness; after self-possession, self-giving. We have to determine to what extent philosophy is justified in seeing this as an element in the constitution of personality. But we should take good note of the fact that in the current usage of the word this aspect is as primitive as the previous one. The very name "person," the Greek *prosôpon,* signifies at the same time that a being has a face of his own, and also that he *faces* other people. A person faces other people, the universe, God; he holds converse with another person, communes or communicates with him according to intellect and affection.[22] But the contrast between openness towards others and sufficiency towards himself which personality implies, is only too apparent. Possession and giving are opposites when it comes to material objects, whose possession by one excludes possession by another, but it is no longer the same when it comes to spiritual personalities. Not only can they give themselves, commune with one another without ceasing to possess themselves, but it is this possession that they have of themselves that permits them to commune with one another, just as the understanding of oneself is, as Max Scheler rightly said, "the first condition requisite in order that a person may be able to make another person understand who he is." [23] Let it not be objected either that human personality is often self-centered, for this refers rather to shortcomings entailed by its connection with individuality and with its material condition than to the very essence of personality. "The human person," says Père de Régnon, "is inclined to refer everything to himself, and to refer himself to himself. I shall leave it an open question whether this is a necessary constituent of his nature or a vicious defect . . . Of God, the opposite is to be believed." [24]

When it is said that God is personal, it seems that with His transcendence what is meant above all is that it is possible to enter into communication, into communion with Him. It is just in this that the God of true philosophy is to be contrasted with the impersonal God of idealism, and even with the God of Aristotle and Plotinus who is indifferent to the world. This prepares the way for the revelation of the God of Abraham who "speaks" to His people, who "governs" them, who enfolds them in His "love." Yet these are characteristics of personality as such. As Père de Régnon profoundly says: " 'Saying' and 'loving' are directed towards a person, and consequently issue from a person, as against 'thinking' and 'willing,' which are acts of nature considered as the principle of activity." [25] If speaking and loving signify communicating oneself to persons, and are characteristics of personality, it seems we can say that the power at least to communicate oneself forms part of the conception of personality.

This explains how when we said that God is personal we meant not only that He infinitely transcends us, but moreover that He knows us and loves us. Whereas divine personality seemed to us just now to be the basis of true morality, it becomes now the foundation of religion, *i.e.* of the connections that unite man to God, since it is the divine personality that makes God infinitely far from us, and at the same time enables us to commune with Him. Because God is a person, we can speak to Him and love Him, just as He speaks to us and loves us. As the divine personality permits us to distinguish true philosophy from false, it now permits us to distinguish true religion from its substitutes. "All spirituality is a dialogue; a spirituality that is addressed to an anonymous, impersonal companion proves itself by that very fact a lying witness." [26]

But it remains none the less true that philosophy knows in a very different manner what the divine personality reveals about incommunicability, and what it reveals about communication and relationship. Under the first aspect, she knows it as a necessity; so this is what she really means when she says that God is personal. Under the second aspect, on the contrary, she knows it only as a possibility. She really knows nothing about communication in God except that which He makes to His creatures by existing. Yet creation, being a strictly contingent fact, and not being in any way required by the divine essence, would not by any means permit us to conclude that it is of God's essence to communicate Himself and thus to make the gift of Himself a constituent element in the divine personality. Once again we reach a limit-problem, which reason puts forward but cannot solve. Only the revelation of the Trinity will provide the answer.

Philosophical statement about God consists, then, in saying with Pseudo-Dionysus that He is all that is, *i.e.* that He possesses in Himself in a pre-eminent fashion the value of all that is. We may comment here that there is often a tendency to identify God with such an aspect of reality. It is thus that Plato ranges God on the side of mind, by contrast with the world of matter. But this is ambiguous. For if it is true that God is *esprit,*[27] it remains true also that the world of bodies is not alien to Him. But He possesses in Himself in a pre-eminent fashion both that which creates the value of mind and that which creates the value of matter. Christianity is not a spiritualism in the Platonic sense of the word, which identifies the divine with the sphere of spirit. But Christianity implies also a materialist aspect. This is of great practical consequence, for it is by not making this sufficiently clear that Christians may well have given the impression to men who have more to do with matter, and who respected its potentialities, that they were strangers to them.

We may make a similar comment on other ideas. It is commonly said that God is immovable, and it is right to say so. The meaning is that God is entirely detached from the vicissitudes of becoming, from change and evolution. But this runs the risk of giving the impression that God is on the side of immobility and security, that He is opposed to novelty, to motion. Yet, if there is perfection in rest, there is also perfection in motion. If on the human level motion is a sign of insufficiency and thus unworthy of God—this only represents a shortcoming. But in God motion exists in its pre-eminent value, as pure act, as intensity of life, as immanent activity. This is what Bergson clearly saw, when he contrasted the becoming of time with the immanent activity of the mind in pure duration.

Here again, Pseudo-Dionysus expresses this uni-

versal analogy with admirable courage. He shows
that it is false to say that God is great, unless we add
that He is small, for there is a perfection in small-
ness, just as there is a perfection in greatness. God
possesses the one quality just as much as the
other. He is as near to what is small as to what is
great. "The Scriptures celebrate God as Great, and
under the mode of Greatness, and yet they also
speak of that divine littleness which is manifested
in a puff of wind." Equally, if it is true that God
possesses the perfection of that which is identical,
He also possesses that which is active. "He is
stable and immobile, dwelling always in the same
place, and yet mobile, since He radiates through all
things." [28]

This amounts precisely to saying that there is no
reality that does not abound pre-eminently in God,
in that all the perfection that it has is a participation of God in the limitations that belong to created
being. Thus what we love in any creature is only
that which is reflected from Him. The whole
world of the soul and the angels is a book that
speaks to us of God and awakes in us a thirst
that only God can slake, for it cannot give us the
fullness of that which it prompts us to desire. "If
the world did not speak so much of you," says
Claudel, "my weariness would not be so great." [29] It
is this search for God among the creatures that are
only His reflection, which is described in the *Con-
fessions* of St. Augustine: "Beauty so old and so
new, late have I loved you. You were within me
and I was outside myself, and there it was that I

sought you; I scattered myself among your works, and I withered at the touch of their beauty; and those things kept me far from you, which would not be themselves if they did not rest in you." [30]

Not only does all being exist pre-eminently in God, but it exists in Him in a sufficient manner, *i.e.* in an absolute fullness that exhausts every possibility. Plato had already noted this feature of divine being, when he said that God is without needs (*anendèès*), *i.e.* that He is absolutely self-sufficing, since He expresses in Himself the fullness of that which is; therefore He can receive nothing, He abides only in Himself. This is the "aseity" which distinguishes Him utterly from the creature, whose essence is to receive its being from another. Equally, God's will is fully satisfied and fulfilled within Himself, in the perfect possession of His fullness. Therefore he who possesses Him possesses all in Him. As Catherine of Genoa says: "He who desires some thing loses what he desires, to know God, who is all things."

But it must be added that all this exists in God in a transcendent manner, *i.e.* that after having asserted that He possesses the being of all things, we must deny it, for God possesses this being in a manner utterly other than that in which He exists in created things; and this manner is entirely inconceivable to us; we can only assert it. He is not the being of all, He is the being who is beyond all, not through essence, but super-essence—according to a word dear to Pseudo-Dionysus—and "the unknowing of that super-essence, which surpasses reason, thought and essence, such should be the object of super-essential science." But this super-essential science is no longer philosophy. Only faith, which is participation in the knowledge of that which God Himself knows, penetrates that darkness and knows God not only as He who is all, but as He who transcends all, not only the same, but the utterly other, not other than love but yet (to use a phrase of Père de Lubac) an otherness of love.

Finally, what philosophy can assert of God is that He is pre-eminently the being in whom the reality of all things is exhausted. But even this assertion will be the source of what we may well call the fundamental difficulty of philosophy, which no philosophy has entirely succeeded in overcoming, without the light of revelation. This difficulty is that, if God exhausts reality in Himself, we cannot see how there can exist and how there does exist any other thing than He. The paradox of philosophy, then, would seem to be that it is caught between two alternatives: either it is an assertion of the sufficiency of reason herself and a negation of God, or else it is an assertion of the sufficiency of God to Himself and a negation of man. But the possibility of the coexistence of God and other things appears to be untenable. This brings us back to the problem of creation, which we must now examine more deeply.

The difficulty is as old as philosophy. We may say that it is *the* philosophical problem. Ancient thought had given two different answers. For Parmenides, only the One exists, and all multiplicity is an illusion. Thus God is affirmed, and the world is denied. This is what is called acosmism. In the Indian tradition it is the doctrine of Sankara, which drives Indian monism in the direction of world-negation. Nothing ever existed but God alone; the rest is a dream from which one wakes, and philosophy is the awakening. In face of acosmism, antiquity offers us another solution, that of pantheism, which, however, is in the last analysis only a less rigorous way of expressing the same concept. Here again creation does not exist, has no proper consistency. It is the unfolding of unity—or, in other words, being, which is one and is God, existing in a collected form, which is God, and in a dispersed form, which is the world. But it is enough for man to recollect himself, to pass from the divine which is in everything to the divine which is in him. The rhythm of the life of man is thus identical with the rhythm of the cosmos, which is for him, too, expansion and contraction. This is the pantheism that in the West found expression in Spinoza.

The nineteenth century put the question differently. The development of the idea of progress led to the assignment of value to becoming, and gave it a positive meaning. Reality is the perpetual arising of creative newness. Yet this appears to be annulled, and progress deprived of all creative value, in that everything super-exists pre-eminently in God. Progress, then, does nothing but rediscover what has always been known, and produce what has always existed. The pre-existence of God seems to empty it of all content, and necessarily leads to a philosophy of the eternal, which is the negation of the value of time. So modern pantheism, reversing the perspective, makes God not He who has always existed, but He who no longer exists. God, the absolute Mind of Hegel, is the end of history. History becomes theogenetics.

We may say that this constitutes the philosophy of the nineteenth century. Hegel gave it an idealist look. Strauss applies it to the history of religion. Becoming materialist with Marx, it retains none the less a religious basis, the idea of man the demiurge of God-humanity. Teilhard de Chardin struggles to provide a version acceptable to Christians, but is only partially successful. We can estimate the extent to which it overflows the banks of systematic philosophy, and has infected the structure of the modern spirit, by reading this passage from Rilke: "Why not prove that God is He who shall come, He who from all eternity must come, that He is the future, the completed fruit of a tree whose leaves we are? Don't you think everything that happens is a beginning? Wouldn't it be God's beginning? What meaning could there be in our quest, if He whom we are looking for belonged already to the past?" [31]

In contemporary philosophy, this fundamental difficulty has found fresh expression in Sartre and Merleau-Ponty. Sartre, metaphysically elaborating the Nietzschean theme of the death of God as the condition for the existence of man, claims in the Preface to his *Descartes* that, existence being identical with creative liberty, man only exists if his free act is an absolute beginning, if no essence precedes existence. *Les Mouches* illustrates the theme in dramatic terms. Oreste only exists when he has killed Agamemnon. Merleau-Ponty in his turn criticizes the Christianity of transcendence, and opposes to it what he calls a Christianity of incarnation, in which God becomes man, not in the Christian sense of the word, by remaining God, but by identifying Himself with man. The existence of a God distinct from man seems to him incompatible with man's existence, for man then becomes an object for God, and this annihilates him. God must therefore exist and man must not exist, or man must exist and God must not exist.

The existentialism of Sartre and Merleau-Ponty removes the obstacle in the sense of affirming man and denying God. It has its exact counterpart in the theology of Karl Barth, who renews the acosmism of Parmenides and Sankara. Taking up the *solus Deus* of Luther, he denounces all claims to human liberty, which seem to him usurpations of the absolute sovereignty of divine liberty. All that God does not work in man is nothingness. There is no knowledge of God except that which God works in the spirit, and any claim to a philosophical knowledge of God is idolatry and illusion. There are no virtues but those that the grace of God works in man, and any idea of merit, of a partnership of God with man in his salvation, is denounced as pride. Man seems to Barth to be unworthy of damnation. Barth's predestinationism leads, paradoxically, to a doctrine of universal salvation. Thus man is despoiled of the last thing that he imagined he could still call his own and subtract from the divine omnipotence—the right to go to hell in his own way. For, as Jouhandeau has well said, hell is the ultimate expression of the value of human liberty. To deny it is to say either that liberty is incapable of resisting effective grace, or that sin is finally so absurd as not even to deserve punishment.

This reference to Barth draws our attention to the most striking aspect of the fundamental difficulty, which is that of the coexistence of the absolute power of God and of man's divine liberty. But this is only an aspect of the problem. Let it be a question of the being of God and of the creature, of the power of God and of human liberty, and we are always brought up against the same difficulty. For if God is all, does all, says all, where is a place to be found for anything else? Metaphysically, we can scarcely see how to justify its existence; we reach an apparently insoluble contradiction. Psychologically, human life seems tasteless, and man feels frustrated, dispossessed, expropriated.

Yet what appears to be a fundamental difficulty turns out to be a sign that we are working in the right direction. For in fact we are brought back to the principles which we stated at the outset. What really characterizes the problem of God, we were saying then, is that it is a limit-problem—that it cannot be mastered by reason; and it is just through this that the reality of God comes to bear upon the problem in that which specifically constitutes Him—*i.e.* in the fact that He transcends reason. Moreover, it is just to this that we are led by the fundamental difficulty. We are brought to the point of making two statements which to all appearances are contradictory. On the one hand, all being loses itself in God; on the other, some being exists outside God. Or again, God determines everything, and yet human liberty determines itself. We are confronted here by a defect in logic, by the impossibility of making our two statements coincide; and they are both of the utmost importance.

Thus the error in all the answers we have found to the problem is just this, that they all fail to accept this opposition, and that they rule out one of the data in the problem. They boil down in the end to the claim of reason to master the difficulty. This is also true of the position of Barth, which returns finally to that of Parmenides, and which involves taking up a philosophical position contrary to analogy. Catholic theology has also made efforts to surmount the problem. We know what an important place the question of grace and liberty has held in its history. But finally these attempts have come to a checkmate; neither Banez nor Molina has found a satisfactory solution. This is a sign that we are really dealing with the mystery of God, which cannot be reduced to entire intelligibility by created mind, but remains fundamentally independent in a realm of sovereign subjectivity.

Yet there is more to be said. What characterizes limit-problems is not only that they cannot be elucidated by reason, but that they compel us to leave the order of discourse, that they drive us towards conversion. Moreover, this is eminently true of the case we are considering. When Sartre and Merleau-Ponty say that the existence of God annihilates man, they are expressing something perfectly real. In that it means that God is the whole of being and that the whole of being comes into God, it means that man possesses nothing of himself; or rather the only thing proper to him is nothingness, for it is only the action of God that arouses him at every single moment from nothingness. Jacques Rivière felt this strongly when he said about sin: "This at least is really mine." He was expressing in this way the fundamental truth that all goodness proceeds from God, just as all happiness does. What God asks of us is to let ourselves love through Him, to agree to receive from Him both being and goodness.

But this is what man refuses to do. For this acceptance is a confession of his utter poverty. It dispossesses him of everything. Moreover, man's passion is to belong to himself. It is repugnant to him to acknowledge his complete dependence, to agree to receive himself at every single moment from another, to leave the entire initiative to God, to be able to hold fast only to something that exists before him and outside him, although this may be more himself than he is. This is why, when his metaphysical perspicacity brings him to acknowledge that all goodness comes from God, he revels in his sins; that all happiness comes from God, he revels in his misery; that all being comes from

God, he revels in nothingness. For this is the only way for him to deny himself to God, if all that is comes from Him, and if the acceptance of being involves the acknowledgment of his dependence.

But the fact that the being that I possess does not belong to me, but is received from another, does not mean, for all that, that this being does not exist. Such is precisely the condition of created being. There is no necessity in it, it is perfectly contingent, it introduces nothing new; and in this sense it is entirely gratuitous, or rather entirely under grace. I am not my own origin. Since my existence began, we have been two. My existence is in its very essence a relationship. I only subsist insofar as I am uttered by another. To acknowledge this fundamental dependence, is simply to ratify what I am. I do not exist except insofar as I am loved. For me, to exist will be to love in my turn, to answer through grace to the action of grace.

Thus created being is not dispossessed of existence, as Sartre claims, but of the appropriation of existence. What I am dispossessed of is my will to self-sufficiency. From the beginning, I am drawn into the cycle of love, of grace and the action of grace. It is impossible for me to separate myself. I enter, then, into the region of "dissemblance," according to the phrase of St. Bernard—*i.e.* of non-being. By a remarkable paradox, it is in my will to sufficiency that I find destruction, while when I acknowledge my insufficiency, I assert my true self. The very notion of creature, which is correlative to the divine aseity, can, then, only be recognized in that

I accept myself existentially as a creature. And that, too, is a limit-notion.

Thus we are led afresh to the idea of creation. It is this that expresses the tension between the existence of a God who exhausts in Himself the possibilities of real being, and the existence of a reality before God which yet has its own existence. But this idea represents a threshold on which philosphical thinking left to itself has never succeeded in standing upright. Gilson has correctly seen in this a category of Christian philosophy, insofar as it is only when relying on revelation that reason has accurately stated it. But even so, the idea remains mysterious. It is affirmed, but not plainly intelligible. It puts forward the two terms, but it does not grasp how they can coexist. Even this intelligibility is the expression, within the scheme of thought, of its reality in the order of existence.

What we said of the fundamental difficulty indicates, then, that it is at the same time the manifestation of the value of reason and of the limits of reason; and that it is just because it is both that it is the right way of putting philosophically the question of God. This applies to philosophy as a whole. It is altogether a threshold. Its supreme act is, therefore, to cross-examine itself, and to show by this means that the cross-examination, which affirms a realm beyond reason, is stipulated by reason. Thus it will appear reasonable to affirm a revelation. A God whom reason dominated would be neither a personal God nor a transcendent God. It is by affirming at the same time that He exists and that He surpasses reason, that reason itself knows Him to be God indeed. A more perfect knowledge of Him would only be His free gift. He is subjective sovereignty, the darkness to which none is able to break through, but which is revealed when and how It wishes. And this is what we call the Revelation.

BIBLIOGRAPHY

Jacques Maritain, *Approches de Dieu,* 1952.

Joseph Pieper, *De l'élément négatif dans la philosophie de St. Thomas, Dieu Vivant,* xx, pp. 35-50.

Pseudo-Dionysus the Areopagite, *Treatise on the Divine Names.*

J. Defever, *La Preuve réélle de Dieu,* 1953.

G. Marcel, *Du Refus a l'invocation,* 1947.

E. Gilson, *The Spirit of Mediaeval Philosophy,* 1936.

Michel E. Sciacca, *L'Existence de Dieu,* 1955.

3

THE GOD OF
the faith

Pascal contrasts the God of Abraham, Isaac and
Jacob with the God of the philosophers and scholars; Barth contrasts the God of Jesus Christ with
the God of the religions. We have tried to show
that the religions and philosophies can achieve a
certain knowledge of the true God. But it remains
true that this knowledge is very imperfect—first in
its manner, because the human mind and soul, when
they are not supported by a Revelation, only reach
halting and conflicting conclusions; and secondly in
content, because what man thus attains is only
what can be known of God through visible things.
But what God is in Himself remains wrapped in
inaccessible darkness, which none can enter by
violence. This is why God is only to be known in
the mystery of His existence through the Revelation,
which He Himself made of Himself, and which is
the object of faith.

Before studying the content of this revelation, we
must first inquire how it is revealed. This indeed
brings us to the crux of what we have to say.
Many men do, in fact, acknowledge God's exist-

ence, but refuse to admit any positive revelation. They do not recognize in the fact of Christianity any original reality. They do not find in the arguments brought forward by Christians a sufficient justification for committing themselves to any absolute conviction. And it is certainly true that the act of faith is not a purely rational conclusion, but carries with it an element of free decision. Still we must try to map out its general direction and its justifying motives.

We said that the object of religion was the knowledge of God through His action in the world. We may add that in this sense religion corresponds to the first Revelation, that which God makes of Himself through creation and providence. This affirmation of an act of God in the cosmos constitutes the first stage. In fact it contrasts the God of religion, who is a living and acting God, with the God of philosophy, who is only a transcendent principle. It is in the extension of this first affirmation that we shall find the starting-point of biblical Revelation. The latter has indeed an essential relationship to divine acts. Here God is not known directly in His essence, but through His manifestations; only these are not, as in the cosmic covenant, the regular pattern of seasonal cycles and the motions of the stars, but single, unique interventions of God in human history, of which the sum-total comprises sacred history or the history of salvation.

Faith is essentially based on divine acts. It consists first of declaring that God intervenes in human history. The facts are those related in the

Bible, which is, strictly speaking, a historical work, but a history not of the deeds of man, but of the deeds of God—for example, the choosing of Abraham, the deliverance of the people of Israel from captivity in Egypt, the dwelling of Yahweh in the temple at Jerusalem, and pre-eminently the Incarnation of the Word and the Resurrection of Christ. Moreover, the chronicle continues into our own times. We still live in the fullness of sacred history. The pouring out of the Spirit at Pentecost inaugurates, in fact, the works of God in the Church. These works are the strictly divine acts known to us as the sacraments, the infallible decisions of the magisterium, conversion and the sanctification of souls. They are achieved by Judgment and the Parousia.

These divine acts, the *mirabilia Dei,* are unique universal acts. The idea of an event is also of the utmost importance. It replaces the cyclical view of the world as an eternally renewed beginning, by a historical view in which time has a meaning. But if each act is unique, they nevertheless make up a whole, a divine plan. The biblical view of the world is that of a history of salvation which has a beginning and an end, and which culminates in the realization of the city of the future. This plan is fulfilled by progressive stages, the ages of the world, which are a divine course of instruction; there is the time of Advent, the preparation, which corresponds to the Old Testament and the choosing of Israel; the incarnation and the resurrection of the Word are the decisive events, the *Kairoi,* which are already accomplished[1]; the time of the Church is that in which the effects of the resurrection of the Word resound throughout mankind; the Judgment will be the definite inauguration of the work of salvation.

At these different stages in the history of salvation, the action of God is expressed through similar works, which clearly show the unity of the plan. Thus the covenant with Abraham and the new covenant in Jesus Christ, the covenant of the Word and the Church and the covenant of baptism, represent the same type of action. Similarly the Flood and the Passion, the Baptism and the Judgment, are parallel acts. We could quote many other examples. The search for these analogies is called typology.[2] They express the general laws of divine action, the ways of God, different from human ways, by which the divine character is revealed in the history of salvation.

Through these works, the living God reveals His methods of action, His customs. It is through these that we are able to know Him. This brings us to what strictly constitutes the biblical revelation of God—the knowledge of the customs of the living God through His acts in the history of salvation. What thus appears to us as God is quite different from what religion or philosophy tell us about Him, and even seems sometimes to contradict it. It is thus that the reading of the Bible, insofar as it describes the works of God, is the source of revelation and the starting-point of faith.

But now a second question arises. We are com-

mitted to the fact of divine acts which make up
sacred history. But how do we know these divine
events? By what right do we declare them? Certainly
history confronts us with outward circumstances that
compose them and are accessible to historical in-
quiry. It is certain that Moses went out of Egypt,
that Jesus was born of Mary, that the Church dis-
tributes the sacraments. But what is strictly divine
in these historical data is not susceptible of being
grasped by the historical method itself. We can recognize these data without having faith. All that
we can assert is that they do not lend themselves
to natural explanation, and that it is therefore reasonable to think that they presuppose a divine intervention.

It is here that we encounter a new element. The
divine character of these events is known through
revelation, *i.e.* through an act which is itself
strictly divine. It is the same God who accomplishes
by His Spirit the works of the history of salvation,
and who, by that same Spirit, gives the understanding of it to His Prophets. Revelation presupposes,
then, not only divine interventions in history, but a
divine act in the spirit of men chosen by God,
which makes them understand these interventions. In
this sense, the very inspiration of the Prophets, and
pre-eminently the revelation of Jesus Christ, as well
as the infallibility of the Church, enter into the
history of salvation of which they are aspects.
"God who, at sundry times and in divers manners,
spoke in times past to the fathers by the prophets,

last of all, in these days hath spoken to us by his Son." [3]

It is, then, the event of the Word of God, revealing God's plan, that is the immediate means of revelation. This Word of God can only be grasped by faith. Indeed, by definition faith has a bearing on the mystery, *i.e.* on God's hidden plan, inaccessible to reason. But if reason cannot grasp it, she can at least recognize its legitimacy. We have already said that philosophy affirmed the existence of a personal God, but could go no farther than this. Indeed the transcendence of God makes Him inaccessible to her capture. But this does not mean that God cannot reveal Himself freely. Revelation thus proceeds from a divine free-will that makes itself known when and how It wishes, and it is clear that, if there is a knowledge of the hidden God, this knowledge can only be brought to light by Revelation.

The all-important question is, then, to know whether God has spoken, *i.e.* where His Word is present in the world. The Christian asserts that the place where the event of God's Word appears is, first of all, God's people. It is in Israel, and through the mediation of the Prophets of Israel, that God first spoke. The Old Testament bears witness to that Word. Afterwards the place of the Word is Christ Himself, who speaks as the Word of God, in whom God's plan is at the same time revealed and fulfilled, who breaks the seven seals of the book that hid from men the secret of their destiny. Finally the place of the Word is the Church, *i.e.* the new people of God, in whom the event of the Word is continued, not insofar as she adds anything to the Word of Christ, who has fulfilled all things, but insofar as she guards and discloses infallible tradition.[4]

Thus, in the last resort, anyone who sets out in search of the Word of God which expounds the Works of God through which the Being of God is revealed, is led to investigate the claims of Scripture, Christ and the Church, which are the sacraments of the Word, the visible species through which we can attain invisible reality. It is through these signs that God speaks to us. If they seem to us to display exceptional features, to present a unity, a sanctity, a fruitfulness that cannot be humanly explained, it will be reasonable to hold fast through them to the Word, which, moreover, speaks directly to the heart of man.

Of all these signs, the manhood of Christ is the most important. In Him appears a pre-eminent holiness, wisdom and power. There is scarcely a man who does not recognize in Him the highest peak of mankind. But it is certainly in other ways that Christ vindicated His divine prerogatives. The whole Gospel reveals Him, less by words than by deeds, as much by His enemies, who treated Him as a blasphemer, as by His disciples, who acknowledged Him to be the Son of God. The entire drama of the Gospel can only be explained in this way. It seems a contradiction to see in Christ, whose pre-eminent moral value is known in other ways, an impostor or a fanatic. It is reasonable to believe Him, when He tells us that He has revealed to us the hidden designs of God.

Faith will be, accordingly, the act by which we affirm the reality of divine events through reliance on the evidence of Jesus Christ. Faith is no longer merely the recognition by reason of her limitations, and the affirmation of mystery, but rather the knowledge of that mystery which appears before us. Faith is the only means of knowing what is beyond knowledge. For the claim of reason to know the mystery comes up against the absolute transcendence of God. At this point, faith demands from reason a confession of her limits, a renunciation of her customary criteria, and a reliance upon a truth of which she lacks evidence. This throws her into a state of confusion. But it is just this confusion that is a sign of the knowledge of the true God, who is He on whom the mind has no longer any hold, and who can only be known through the witness that He bears of Himself.

Moreover, faith seems formidable to man because it involves the acceptance of his dependence and the abandonment of his self-sufficiency. Thus faith reaches him in his will-to-belong; she puts him at the mercy of another. Some writers of the present day criticize Christians for adopting a comfortable attitude, for establishing themselves in a certainty that does without seeking and casts away anguish. But in reality, faith does not provide such a convenient attitude. What they fear fundamentally is just that this irruption of God into their lives may be the occasion of losing themselves, and may involve them in terrible adventures. The problem of faith is the concrete form which even the problem of God takes in the fact of revelation. It is a sign of man's being confronted with the reality of the living God in His awe-inspiring exigency.[5]

Thus we should try to place the realm of faith beyond that of religion and philosophy. It differs, first of all, by its object, which is the showing-forth of God through the plan of salvation. It differs also by its manner, which is that of reliance upon the testimony of the Word of God, such as is expressed through Scripture, Christ and the Church. It differs finally by its content. Indeed it is faith alone that introduces us to the knowledge of God in His hidden mystery, in His sovereign reality. This revelation, we have said, is that which God makes of Himself through His Word in history. First of all, then, we shall consider what we know of God in His relationship to the world of salvation; here we shall deal with those divine customs of which we spoke above. Then we shall see how the existence of the Trinity of Persons reveals Itself likewise through Its works. Only after that shall we see how faith, becoming light, leads to a grasping of God the Three in One in His mysterious essence.

Just as the cosmic idea of God is known through the creation, so the biblical God is known through the covenant. This is the essential feature of the action of God in the Bible. The Hebrew

word *b'rith,* which designates it, means in its profane sense a treaty juridically ratified by an oath
and creating a bond between two individuals or
two communities. Among ancient peoples, this covenant was often sanctioned by a rite which consisted
of the two contracting parties exchanging their
blood, as a symbol of kinship with one another.
Later, in place of this rite was substituted the sacrifice of an animal, which was divided into two
halves, between which the two contracting parties
passed, and of which they each consumed a share.

It is to these ancient customs that the Bible gave
expression, applying them to the relationship between God and His chosen people. The covenant
means, then, the establishment by God of a bond between Himself and the people He has chosen. The
people of Israel is His people, and He is the God
of Israel. By virtue of this covenant, God under-
takes to protect the chosen people; He binds Himself to them in a permanent fashion. The covenant
is sanctioned by a rite which recalls the profane
covenants of the past. At the time when the covenant is first concluded with Abraham, we see Jehovah
commanding him to take a heifer, a goat, a ram and
a turtle-dove, to divide them and place the pieces side
by side. "Now when the sun had set and it was
dark, a smoking oven and a fiery torch passed
between the pieces." [6] In the same way, at the time
of the renewal of the covenant on Sinai, Moses
sacrificed oxen; then he "took half of the blood,
and put it in large bowls; the other half he
splashed on the altar . . . Then he took the blood

and sprinkled it on the people, saying, This is the blood of the covenant, which the Lord has made with you . . ." [7] It is to this rite that Christ will refer when He says, after sharing with His disciples the cup full of wine transubstantiated in His blood: "This is the cup of my blood, the blood of the New Covenant."

Through all the Old Testament texts which describe it, the Covenant displays one remarkable feature. It constitutes an irrevocable commitment on the part of God, who takes the entire initiative in it. This commitment is not, strictly speaking, two-sided. If it carries obligations on the part of the people, it is not conditional upon the fulfilment of these obligations. The people can withdraw from the benefits offered by God's promise, but He can only agree to their being revoked. The faithfulness of God is not at the mercy of the unfaithfulness of man. This is what St. Paul wished to point out when he translated the Hebrew *b'rith,* not by *synthêkê,* contract, but by *diathêkê,* which the Latin itself renders by "Testament." The expression "Old Testament" signifies, then, an irrevocable covenant arising from a unilateral commitment. No doubt this is also shown by the fact that, in the rite of the covenant with Abraham, only fire, the symbol of God, passes between the sacrificial animals.

These features of the Covenant reappear in every period in the history of salvation, showing that it is indeed a question of a characteristic procedure of the living God. Already, before the covenant with Abraham, the covenant with Noah was a sign of

God's irrevocable commitment to respect the cosmic order, despite the sins of men, and never again to ordain a Flood. In the fullness of time, the Incarnation of the Word is to be the new, eternal Covenant. Through it, the Word of God is to be irrevocably united with human nature, once for all and for ever, establishing thus between the human and the divine nature a living communion such that nothing could be more intimate. Henceforth, whatever the sins of men might be, they could never untie this bond. The Church in her turn, being the community of the New Covenant, receives from the Word, who is her Bridegroom, the good things that are His—holiness, infallibility—in an irrevocable manner, so that the idea that the Church might be forsaken by God is impossible. Every Christian in his turn, on entering into the New Covenant by baptism, is the object of a commitment by God, which gives him a title to God's grace. He may withdraw from the benefit of this commitment, but the latter, which is called the baptismal character, cannot be revoked.

Thus the Covenant introduces us to the revelation of the living God with all His mystery and all His paradoxicality. For the Covenant does not proceed by rational exigency; on the contrary, it is disconcerting to reason. It constitutes the heart of God's revelation in the Old Testament. If Holiness expresses what it is in itself, the Covenant makes it known in its relationship with the world. Through it, God reveals a number of characteristics, which define the God of the Bible and strictly constitute

biblical theology—truth, justice, love. These characteristics are often misunderstood, because they are
not interpreted according to their biblical, but according to their popular meaning. Their elucidation
is one of the essential tasks of the knowledge of
God.

The first is truth. The Hebrew word is *emet*.
This word has been translated into Greek as
alètheia, and into Latin as *veritas*. But its meaning
is quite different from that which the Greek and
Latin words have in philosophical usage. For the
Greeks, truth is essentially the transparency of a
thing to the mind. It is, according to the scholastic
definition, the *adaequatio rei et intellectus*. Its symbol
is light. Moreover the very word *alètheia* undoubt-
edly means "unveiling." Thus the criterion of
truth is evidence. But the word *emet* is oriented in
a quite different direction. The root to which it is
attached refers to the solidity of something from
which one receives support. Thus it means the pillar
on which a building rests; it refers to the support
that a child receives when resting in his mother's
arms; it refers to the support that was given to
Moses by the two men who held up his arms while
he prayed on the mountain with arms outstretched.[8]

In the moral sense, the word refers to the faithful servant, on whom reliance can be placed. We
see from this the meaning that it will take when
applied to God. It will designate Him as the one
on whom man can lean with all his weight, because He is true and faithful. We see the transformation that this gives to the idea of truth. Its

foundation is no longer the evidence of something known, but the veracity of the testimony that supports knowledge. The means of access to truth is, then, no longer reason, but faith. To believe is to lean with all one's weight on the Word of God, and this is not an inferior mode of knowledge, but on the contrary the very core of knowledge. For it is true that reason does not attain the last essential realities. These are only known by testimony. And faith, which is a higher mode of certainty, is also the means of access to higher realities.

We see now the importance of this point. Insofar as we approach biblical realities through Greek conceptions of truth, it is clear that we shall be out of countenance. This is precisely what many minds experience. They apply to revealed realities the criterion of rational evidence, which is the only criterion they know. But these realities are not to be grasped in this way. They are not intrinsically evident to reason; and it is only a step from this to denying that they can be the object of certainty. But it is a mistake to conceive this certainty on the pattern of rational and scientific knowledge. The certainty of faith, founded on testimony, is a certainty of absolute value. This is already true on the human scale, where the essential certainties of existence, the love of others for us, the reality of historical events, are only known by testimony.[9] To consider that they are accordingly not susceptible of absolute certainty, is to yield to morbid doubt.

We shall see, in fact, that the criterion of evidence only makes use of the value of the lower world of material things; as soon as we reach the level of persons, we come up against the limits of reason. The property of persons, as Scheler well said, is silence. They can only be known if they reveal themselves; and they only reveal themselves through love. On the level of testimony, truth leaves the world of things to enter the world of persons. It becomes a sign of the relationship that links them together, of their inter-subjectivity; it is the mark of their communication; it brings them into communication with one another; it withdraws them from solipsism and idealism. Thus truth assumes a moral character. Bearing witness commits the entire personality, insofar as it is responsible. Lack of truth is no longer called error, but lying.[10]

If this is how things are on the level of persons, it is clear that it is even more the case with God. The claim to make God an object which the mind can capture is a blasphemous claim. God is sovereign subjectivity. This is the meaning of his proper name in the Bible, Yahweh, which must be translated not as "I am He Who is," i.e. being, but as "I am That I am," i.e. sovereignly independent within being, personal and living being. Henceforth God can only be known if He reveals Himself. This is why revelation is the means of access to the knowledge of the hidden God. This revelation is expressed by the Word, which is the testimony that God gives of Himself. This Word bears within it the guarantee of pre-eminent divine perfection. So we can lean upon it with all our weight. That weight is faith, and that absolute solidity of the revealing Word is precisely what the Bible calls *emet*. It is truth.

This is expressed concretely in the Bible by the fact that the symbol of truth is not light, as with the Greeks, but rock. Light contrasted with darkness indicates the world of good as against the world of evil. But it is rock that indicates God as Truth. It appears particularly in the song of Moses in *Deuteronomy*, which was a sort of catechism for Judaism at the time of Christ:

> *The Rock, how faultless are his deeds:*
> *How right all his ways!*
> *A faithful God without deceit,*
> *How just and upright he is."* (32:4)

The Rock thus refers to the unshakable firmness of the Word of God, on which it is legitimate for man to play out the destiny of his intellect and to commit that of his life. Indeed it is a firmer foothold for man than man himself: "Cursed be the man that trusteth in man." [11] At this point, truth is united with holiness. For it is because God is infinitely holy, because He is sovereign perfection, that man has the right to put unconditional faith in Him.

We shall see that the word by which man acknowledges this firmness of the Word of God comes from the same root as *emet*. This word is one of the Hebrew words which the liturgy of the Church has borrowed from that of the synagogue, one which we use every day, the word *amen*. To repeat it, is to say of the Word of God: "This is

solid and I believe in it." It is this *Amen* that the
Angels pronounce before the throne of Christ in
the Book of *The Apocalypse*. But still more is it
the very name of Christ Himself, insofar as He
is the faithful witness on whom our whole faith
rests: "These things saith the Amen, the faithful
and true witness, who is the beginning of the creation of God." [12]

The truth of God is, then, the sovereign veracity
of the testimony by which He enables us to know
the mystery, *i.e.* at the same time His hidden life
and His hidden plan upon earth. But this does not
exhaust the content of the biblical *emet*. For the
Word of God is not only the manifestation of a
truth; it is also the promise of good things. It is
even in this very way that it is revealed in the
covenant. God appears there to Abraham as He
who announces good things to come. This promise
of God is irrevocable. And that is precisely what
the wor*d emet* means. It expresses that God's faithfulness to His promises is absolutely sure, and that
we can lean unreservedly on His Word, not only
insofar as it reveals what is, but as it promises
what shall be. God is thus a Rock, in that we can
put our whole confidence in Him and be sure of His
support:

> "*You are my rock and my fortress;*
> *For your name's sake you will*
> *Lead me and guide me.*" [13]

God appears here no longer as truth, but as
faithfulness; and this faithfulness corresponds not

to faith, but to hope. Hope is not like the *elpis* of the Greeks, an attitude before an uncertain future. It is the paradoxical affirmation of the happy issue of the time, an entering into possession expected in the future. But again this affirmation is not founded upon any optimism whatever, but on the immanent necessity of things. It rests entirely upon the Word of God, who "meaning more abundantly to shew to the heirs of the promise the immutability of his counsel, interposed an oath: That by two immutable things, in which it is impossible for God to lie, we may have the strongest comfort, who have fled for refuge to hold fast the hope set before us." [14]

The problem of God's justice raises similar questions to that of His truth. Here again we are in the presence of an idea borrowed from current language, which in this case served to translate a biblical category, the *tsedeq*. For lack of a precise study of this word, and therefore of the word "justice" in biblical usage, we see what confusion we are in danger of incurring. Moreover, the existence of these confusions is not a myth. How many social theories have claimed the authority of that saying of Christ: "Blessed are they which do hunger and thirst after justice"! [15] What confused ideas are suggested to the majority of minds by a sentence like: "Seek ye first the kingdom of heaven and its justice"! Lack of precision in elucidating these basic categories of biblical theology may have the gravest consequences. This is why we think it worth while to emphasize such points.

Among the Ancients we find a current conception of justice. The Greeks call it *dikè*, the Latins *iustitia*. Its essential purpose is to insure that the right, *ius*, of everyone should be respected, that everyone should have rendered to him what is his due. This justice is the foundation of human societies. It is also the imperious demand of the human soul. (Nothing shocks a child more than injustice.) It easily takes the form of an equalitarian claim, in protest against the inequality of conditions and as a demand that all should be treated equally. In every way, it seems to require that there should be a due proportion between merit and retribution.

But if we confront the reality of the world with this conception of justice, we are compelled to state that it implies a complete contradiction. I am not thinking here of social injustices, for which the responsibility can be allotted to man, but of what one may call natural injustices. How can we speak of justice in a world where some children are born weak and others with every advantage, where there are innocent people overwhelmed with misfortune and criminals flourishing with impunity? If we apply to such a world the criteria of human justice, and if we summon God before the tribunal of that justice, He could not but be condemned. This is what rightly makes an author like Camus refuse to accept a world constructed in such a way, for he can see no other answer to it than revolt. Attempts to justify God seem still more perilous, for they end inevitably in a checkmate. How can we dare to claim that there is a relationship between virtue and goodness, between vice and misfortune, when the contradictions are so glaring? Moreover, the Bible itself has refuted in advance, through the mouth of Job, all attempts of this kind.[16] They end, besides, in the worst Pharisaism. For if prosperity necessarily accompanies virtue, it is also its criterion, and the fortunate of this world could then settle down with a good conscience and calmly despise the unfortunate, regarding their misery as a just punishment. In the practical sphere, the triumph of force would be identified with the triumph of right, and the conquered people would necessarily be the guilty people. We see the dangerous providentialism to which all this would lead.[17]

But at the bottom of this there is a fundamental ambiguity. For God's justice, according to the Bible, has nothing in common with the commutative justice that governs relationships between men, and the mistake lies precisely in wishing to apply such a criterion to the relationship between God and men. If the facts themselves were not already startling enough to arouse our suspicions and put us on our guard against an immediate scandal, the teachings of the Gospel would be sufficient to enlighten us in this matter. A parable like that of the workmen in the last hour is indeed a flat contradiction of the human conception of justice, and constitutes in man's eyes a complete outrage. It puts forward in principle the right of God to treat men with the most perfect inequality, and without taking any account of the difference between their respective rights.

But what Christ meant to show us here is precisely that the fundamental error in our idea of the relationship between man and God was to imagine that man had any rights before God whatever. This was the mistake of the Pharisees, who claimed to be treated according to their merits and brought their demands before God. But it is this claim on the part of man that must be entirely overruled. Man has nothing except what he receives as a completely free gift, and he therefore has nothing at all on which he could base a claim. Accordingly he cannot complain if he is treated differently from others. God demands sovereign freedom in the designation of His gifts. Perhaps in the end we shall be "up on the deal", and it would be better for us in the last resort to put our trust in merciful love, rather than to make a stand on our supposed merits.

But shall we not fall into the opposite idea of an arbitrary God? The Bible teaches us just the reverse. What it denounces is man's claim to judge according to the standards of his own justice. We come back to what we said above on the subject of reason. A God who was just, after the style of man, would not be the transcendent, hidden God. But there *is* justice in God. That justice, if it is at first disconcerting for man, if it seems strange to him and stupefies him, is in reality wholly excellent. The God of the Bible thus forces man to leave his own ways, which are short and

narrow, and enter the ways of God, which are
infinitely wiser and more merciful. This requires of
him that conversion, that decentralization from himself, which is—as we have already stated several
times—the very sign of an encounter with the
living God.

It is this justice of God which is the *tsedeq* of the
Bible. It does not consist of the fact that God owes
something to man, but in what He owes to Himself.
Justice is thus a continuation of truth. It consists
for God of keeping His commitments and thus
showing His faithfulness. It is the fulfilment of
His promises that attests God's justice. This is
how we should interpret certain otherwise obscure
passages in the New Testament. When Christ says
that He came to fulfill all justice, this does not
mean that He came to establish a just wage or a
just peace, but to keep the promises made to
Abraham by saving captive humanity. When Christ
tells us that the Comforter "will convince the world
of sin, and of justice, and of judgment . . . because
I go to my Father," [18] He means that by His glorious exaltation He reveals the success of the divine
plan and denounces the error of those who have not
believed in Him.

Justice often presents in this way an eschatological character. If truth accompanies the promise,
justice appears in its fulfilment. It provides a verifi-
cation. It is in this sense that justice draws near to
the Kingdom as an object of expectation, and it is
in this sense that we should understand texts like:
"Blessed are they which do hunger and thirst after

justice." This means that those who have believed in the divine promises are finally right and will see them fulfilled. So also when Christ tells His followers to "seek the kingdom of heaven and its justice." Justice and the Kingdom are one and the same thing. They are the order of things in which God's plan triumphs. So again when it is a question of those who "are persecuted for justice's sake." God's justice is not defined with reference to man. It is the faithfulness of love to itself. We see from this why the order that it establishes is better. To believe that God is just, is to believe that it is He who will finally be right, despite all appearances, that He will make His cause prevail, that "He will be the strongest," as Claudel's Joan of Arc says—and that He will thus insure the wellbeing of those who have believed in Him.

God's justice is completed in Jesus Christ, for it is in Him that God fulfils His promise. This dominates the whole Christian outlook, which is faith in a salvation freely given to sinners and not legally merited by the just: "But now the justice of God without the law is made manifest . . . upon all them that believe in him: for there is no distinction: for all have sinned, and do need the glory of God; being justified freely by his grace, through the redemption, that is in Christ Jesus." [19] God's justice, far from being proportioned to human merits, is shown on the contrary, as St. Paul says, by the fact that God has declared His justice "for the remissions of former sins," [20] that the success of His plan is not at the mercy of man—and that the condition on which we may benefit from it is faith.

Thus man's righteousness is not the condition, but the consequence of God's action. It is this alone that justifies. The righteous man is he whom God declares and renders such. It is God's justice that thus provides the measure of man's, and not the other way about. The only thing that is required of man is faith. But the faith of which St. Paul speaks is not what Luther wished it to mean. It is not only confidence in the justice of God, in His ultimate victory, but the conforming of one's life to the will of God. It is not enough to be baptized in order to be saved, any more than it was enough to belong to the people of Israel in order to enter into their inheritance.[21] But the righteous man is he in whom is found justification by the fruits of life and by holiness, and who thus bears witness to a justice that does not derive from himself, but comes from God. He is not only one who believes in the fulfilment of promises, but is one in whom they are fulfilled.[22]

Thus we are brought back to the popular idea of justice, insofar as it expresses in human relationships a respect for the rights of the individual. We have said that biblical justice had in substance nothing in common with human justice, and this is quite true. But biblical justice implies, nevertheless, the duty of man to respect and promote the person of his fellow-man. Only this obligation does not proceed ultimately from the rights of persons as such, but from the fact that this respect for persons is the expression of the will of God. It is, then, obedience to God, the acknowledgment of the charter of the covenant, that implies a certain order of human society.[23] Here again, justice will be defined, not by reference to the claims of man, but to the will of God. This is why Christian justice must surpass that of the scribes and Pharisees, in that it is identified with charity.

To the truth and justice of God, Scripture adds His love, *hesed*. Here again it is important to establish the content of the biblical notion through its relationship with the popular use of the word. But we shall not need to insist on this so much, as an abundant literature has dealt with the question in our time. The great pioneer in this field is Max Scheler, in his *Nature et Formes de la Sympathie* and his *L'Homme du ressentiment*. He has shown the contrast between the Platonic *erôs,* which is the impulse of the imperfect towards the perfect in search of fulfilment, and the biblical *agapè,* which has a person as its object and compels him to will for himself the good. Thus *erôs* appears as egocentric and confronts the world of things; hence it recalls idealist knowledge, which is relationship with being, insofar as it is inward to me through thought. *Agapè,* on the other hand, is essentially disinterested, a connection with the person of others insofar as they exist outside myself; it dwells on the level of persons.

Scheler pointed out particularly that by contrast

with *erôs,* which is a sign of poverty of being—it appears as such in Plato—*agapè* is a sign of full-ness of being. It is a movement of generosity and giving, which descends from him that has to him that has not. This is why it appears at its maximum in the love of the poor. But for all that, it implies no complicity with misery, as Nietzsche complains that it does. What it reaches, in fact, is not values, but persons. It only affects the person of someone who is unhappy in order to arouse values in him. It is at the same time love of persons and love of values. In this respect it is not opposed to *erôs,* but rather integrates it, and purifies its ego-centricity.[24] It is, as Père de Montcheuil well says, "connection with the appetite of being in others." Thus it overcomes the pseudo-problem of pure love. Disinterestedness does not consist in not wanting values for myself, but in wanting them at the same time for others.

This analysis of Scheler's has not been superseded. Anders Nygren has made it the basis of a force-ful study in biblical theology. But if Nygren's documentation is useful, his criticism is less just than Scheler's. In particular, Nygren overestimates the contrast between *agapè* and *erôs,* and in his wish to eliminate *erôs* from the biblical perspective, he reduces *agapè* to a descending movement from rich to poor. Thus he is led to find *agapè* in the pure state only in a few texts of St. Paul. Even St. John seems to him suspect. But this is to risk bringing us back to the Nietzschean view and losing sight of the fact that *agapè* has as its object not only the person, but also value in the person, and that it is pleasure in existing good as well as the conferring of good where it does not exist.

It is in this perspective that we are to place the biblical *hesed*. In its secular meaning the word refers not to a feeling but to an act. It means the establishment of a bond of covenant implying mutual[25] help. Applied to God, it means one of the aspects through which He reveals Himself in the covenant, *i.e.* the establishment of good things in common. It is the objective aspect of love which thus appears first, insofar as it constitutes a permanent kinship implying mutual services. Such was the covenant between Yahweh and Israel. It involves an exchange of oaths. The people knows that it can count on Yahweh's help. The *hesed* is a commitment. It arises from the will and not from affective sources. And Yahweh must also be able to count on His people. We see that *hesed* is closely related to *emet,* in that it implies faithfulness. But it is faithfulness seen in the aspect of the communication of good things.

This explains how the bond between the people and God is expressed by the symbol of the various forms of the family community, which fulfills the type of enduring kinship. Sometimes the image is that of father and son:

> *"When Israel was a child, and I loved*
> *him,*
> *And I called my son out of Egypt."* [26]

> *"Sion said, The Lord hath forsaken*
> *me,*
> *And the Lord hath forgotten me.*
> *Can a woman forget her infant?"* [28]

But the most frequent theme is that of marriage. Yahweh is the Bridegroom, and Israel the bride. Osee develops this in some fine passages, where all the aspects we have mentioned are taken up:

> *"I will betroth thee to me for ever;*
> *And, I will betroth thee to me in jus-*
> *tice* (tsedeq),
> *And in judgment, and in lovingkind-*
> *ness* (hesed), *and in mercies.*
> *And I will betroth thee to me in faith*
> (emunah) :
> *And thou shalt know I am the*
> *Lord."* [29]

The *Song of Songs* gives incomparable expression to this love of Yahweh and His people.

But if the description of Yahweh's love for Israel borrows imagery from human society, it presents the appropriate features of the theology of the covenant. We have said that the characteristic of the covenant was to be unilateral, in the sense that God's commitment is unconditional. This is expressed, first of all, by the fact that He takes the whole initiative. His is a creative love, which arouses persons in order to bring them good things.

Their goodness is not the cause, but the result of His love. Thus He reveals His whole freedom. It has been well noted by Nygren that this sharply contrasts biblical love with Platonic love. Unilateral love is to dominate the whole of the Christian theology of grace, according to which man does nothing but respond to the action of God within Him.

This concept appears above all in the New Testament. The love of God, *agapè,* is revealed in the fact that the Word of God, having put on human nature, is to give His life for sinful man. He does not wait for man to turn towards Him, but goes forth to seek him. Grace comes before conversion. It is in this connection that St. John and St. Paul give the strict definition of *agapè:* "In this is charity: not as though we had loved God, but because He hath first loved us," [30] and "God commendeth His love (*agapè*) towards us; because when as yet we were sinners, Christ died for us." [31] The love of God is thus the principle and origin of all grace and all good.

But if the love of God is unilateral, in that the living kinship which it establishes is not at the mercy of man's infidelities, it remains true that the enjoyment of this kinship requires an answering love on the part of man. For God's love is a jealous love. This is one of those phrases the anthropomorphism of which often shocks modern man. It is true that it can be taken in the wrong way. There is a meaning of the word "jealousy", indeed, which indicates the impatience that we feel on see-

ing other people enjoying good things which we
ourselves lack. In this sense jealousy is a sin, and
of course incompatible with God.[32] But the Bible
uses the word "jealousy" in the sense of the demand made by the relationship between husband
and wife, which prevents them from allowing the
love once given to be ever taken away. In this
sense, jealousy is the very sign of conjugal faithfulness in all its nobility.

Applied to the relationship between Yahweh and
Israel, God's jealousy is a continuation of the
nuptial imagery of *hesed*. It means that God will
not allow to be given to any other than Himself
that absolute homage of love which we call worship. This is why in the Old Testament God's
jealousy appears, for the first time, in relation to
the condemnation of idols: "You shall not carve
idols for yourselves in the shape of anything in the
sky above or on the earth below . . . For I, the
Lord, your God, am a jealous God . . ."[33] God's
jealousy appears here as a concrete sign of monotheism. It means that God does not allow any creature
to receive the honor that is due to Him alone. This is
why the unfaithfulness of His people, with whom
He is united "as a pure virgin," to use St. Paul's
phrase, is an act of adultery that arouses His
wrath.[34]

Thus what is revealed through God's jealousy is
the intensity, the violence of the divine love, in all
its irrational and mysterious reality. This anthropomorphic expression, which scandalizes the Pharisees,
seems to be one of those which are introduced

very early in the mystery of God. It brings us into contact, indeed, with what Guardini calls "the seriousness of divine love," *i.e.* the paradoxical, overwhelming fact that God attaches importance to our love, and so puts Himself in some way at our mercy. How far this is from the Olympian self-sufficiency of the God of reason! The living God seems as if committed to His creation, as if in some way jointly answerable with it. This solidarity is expressed in the essential act of His love, that of the Incarnation. Hence the relationship between man and God takes on a tragic significance. God's jealousy reveals to us the price that God sets on every human soul. He gives to His love the character of a personal bond.

Thus, through His mighty works, the living God reveals His hidden nature. He no longer appears as the pre-eminent realization of the values of men, of their absolute perfection. On the contrary, His ways disconcert us. But it is just at this point that He imposes upon us His objective reality. He compels our reason and our will to forsake their own ways and adjust themselves to His. He brings us into the mysterious sphere that is His own. And so the knowledge of the living God, as revealed in His works, leads the mind progressively towards the knowledge of God as He is in Himself.

The biblical term that defines the nature of God in His own mystery is that of holiness. The Hebrew word *qodesh*, which is translated as *sanctus*, implies the idea of separation. It serves, first of all, to indicate all that is set apart, reserved for the worship of God. This meaning is not specifically Hebraic; the distinction between sacred and profane is common to all religions. But, starting from this cultic meaning, the term "holiness" comes to stand in the Old Testament for the divine being itself, insofar as it is essentially separated from everything else, and is entirely other, the transcendent. This change appears chiefly in *Isaiah*.[35] It is in the vision that opens the ministry of this Prophet that God reveals Himself as the Thrice Holy, hidden within the sanctuary and surrounded by the choir of seraphim.[36]

The holiness of God expresses, first of all, His sovereign reality. In Him, being is manifested in all its intensity. This sovereign reality appears in the Bible through the fact that man cannot bear its weight when he approaches it. It is no longer a question of a metaphysical statement, but of the existential encounter with the living God. The density of His existence is such that man feels crushed by it. This is religious experience in its crude, elemental state, such as the Bible describes in the words: "No man can see God and live." The *Book of Job,* after recounting the wonders of God in the universe, which are viewed with astonishment by men, concludes by saying:

> "Lo, these are but the outlines of his
>   ways,
> And how faint is the word we hear?
> But the thunder of his power
> Who can understand?" (26:14)

Thus the whole creation is only "a little portion," a faint murmur, in comparison with that which is the Lord Himself. Yet already we can scarcely bear its glory. The beauty of the world is sometimes so intense that it alarms us. But if it were the real Beauty of God that was unveiled before us in itself, and not through shadows and reflections, it would be like thunder bursting our eardrums. Rilke felt this keenly when he wrote with regard to the angels:

> "If one of them suddenly
> Held me within his heart, I should
>   fall dead
> At his too mighty being, because
>   beauty
> Is the beginning of the terrible." [37]

Beauty corresponds to the angelic sphere. It is true that the angels have a bond with the cosmos, and that art contains a daimonic element—not necessarily demonic or demoniac, for it may also be angelic. But that beauty, Rilke feels, would be beyond endurance, the being of an angel, "too mighty." What would it be like, then, if God Himself pressed with His whole weight upon the heart?

This weight of God upon the heart has a name; it is mystical experience. The mystic is one who experiences the reality of the living God. But he cannot bear it—and that is exactly what he feels. The brightness of the divine light is too intense for sight to endure without perishing. This is why St. John of the Cross says that it is darkness. The abyss of God is too dazzling for sight to fathom, and this is why Gregory of Nyssa speaks of being dazzled by the divine essence.[38] St. Francis Xavier felt this insupportable weight when he exclaimed in the midst of his ecstasy: "Enough! Enough!" The heart of St. Theresa burst beneath the weight, as she tells us in her memoirs. The physical phenomena that accompany mystical union refer to this unendurable experience. Already the Bible shows us Abraham falling into a kind of mystical slumber, which we should call suspension of consciousness, when the glory of God drew near to him.

Holiness appears, therefore, in its first aspect, as the positive side of what philosophy showed us negatively. The transcendence which philosophy demonstrated consisted of saying that God was nothing that man is, but it did not say what God was. It is the same reality of transcendence, in its living experience, that holiness reveals, and, correlatively, it leads man to know himself as a creature. "By contrast with the power of which we have a presentiment outide us," as Otto rightly says, "the sense of being a creature becomes clear within us in proportion to our sense of self-effacement, the sense of our annihilation in proportion to the consciousness of being nothing but dust and ashes. This numinous sense forms, so to speak, the raw material of religious humility." [39] St. Catherine of Siena gave the most exact account of this experience in the words that were spoken to her by Christ: "I am That I am, thou art that which is not."

Indeed, religious experience concurs here with

metaphysical reality. We come back to the divine aseity, but expressed in terms of intensity, and to human contingency as the annihilation of the creature by divine reality. But at the same time the experience of this annihilation seems to us not to be one of destruction, but of conversion. Before the sovereign reality of the divine being, the mind becomes aware of the unreality of everything else. The glory of God, by manifesting itself, extinguishes the light of creatures. This does not mean that they have no glory but that which they receive from God. What is destroyed is only the lying world in which the light of creatures hides the divine light from the human mind. The world with its countless flickerings of pleasure prevents us from contemplating the great night sky in which the mind is really immersed. Things now return to their proper places; God occupies the center, and all else is banished to the circumference.

But while making an irruption into the world, while drawing near to the soul of man, God remains He who is altogether other. This unwonted feature of the situation causes the mind to lose its bearings, for it has no landmark by which it can place this mysterious reality, no foothold by which it can ascend to it. The soul experiences the fundamental religious condition of fear, the *pavor* of the Latins, the *awe* of the English, the *thambos* of the Greeks. This has been brilliantly analyzed by Otto: "The mysterious, in the religious meaning of the word, in truth *mirum,* is, to use the phrase which is perhaps the most accurate, the altogether other, that which is alien to us and disconcerts us, that which is entirely outside things as they are commonly understood, well known and familiar. The mysterious appears in complete contrast to the common run of things, and by that very fact fills us with paralyzing astonishment." [40]

Here we encounter "the terrible," of which Rilke was saying that the beautiful is only its beginning, the *tremendum,* which the *Dies irae* reveals as *"rex tremendae maiestatis."* The terror described here has nothing to do with ordinary fear, with dread of punishment. It belongs to the metaphysical order, and expresses the total disproportion between the greatness of God and the capacity of the human mind. This grandeur, this immensity, which overflows man in every dimension, is called majesty. Its approach throws man into confusion, and distracts him like a compass needle in the neighborhood of a magnet whose potential is too powerful:

> *"And he shall go into the clefts of the*
> *   rocks,*
> *And into the holes of stones*
> *From the face of the fear of the*
> *   Lord,*
> *And from the glory of his majesty,*
> *When he shall rise up to strike the*
> *   earth."* [41]

Thus the approach of the mystery takes on its full religious meaning. It comes to undermine man's claim to be enclosed within his own limits, to be sufficient to himself. It compels him to recognize the precarious and threatened nature of his existence. It decentralizes man from himself, and makes him forsake his accustomed ways. No longer is it simply a question of the necessary statement of transcendence, but of the formidable presence of that transcendence in all its awe-inspiring reality. There is even a paradox in the revelation of the biblical God, for He is present as mystery in the heart of the profane world, present as mystery within man, carrying him away, yet only bearing down upon him in order to change him.

This makes it clear why the experience of the holy, the fear of God, in the sense defined above, is the essential basis of genuine religion. It safeguards, in fact, the transcendence of God at the heart of His immanence. It is the unbreakable barrier that stops genuine religion from turning into pantheism. It preserves the gulf that separates Creator from creature, at the heart of the gift which the Creator makes of Himself to the creature. It reveals the freedom of God's gift, by showing that the divine life is in man an alien reality, and not a natural property. It gives him also his full value, for the value of God's free gift is only seen if first we have caught a glimpse of what God is in Himself. It utterly forbids religion to stoop to the least familiarity, and admonishes us to come forward with the utmost reverence.

But it remains true that the characteristic of strangeness, if it faithfully expresses the essence of holiness—which really means apartness—is far from exhausting its content. This is revealed on the scale of being, not on that of goodness. But holiness expresses also transcendence within the order of value; it is a sign of the infinite excellence of God, which He lays upon man not only as an overwhelming fullness of existence, but also as sovereign perfection, from which man cannot withhold unconditional respect, and which arouses in him the fundamental religious attitude, which is that of adoring worship.

This again has been well described by Otto: "The sense of *sanctus* appears as the sense of something that commands incomparable respect, something in which one must recognize supreme objective value. Terror in the presence of divine holiness does not coincide with mere dread of absolute power and the *tremenda maiestatis,* in face of which no other attitude is possible than that of blind and abject obedience. *Tu solus sanctus* is not the cry of fear, but a salutation of praise overflowing with veneration; it is not the mere stammering of man in the presence of one who represents superior power, but it is also the expression of man desiring to recognize and exalt that which possesses a value beyond his comprehension. What he exalts is not the absolute power that confers worthiness upon exigencies and constrains man within limits, but it is the power which in its essence possesses the capacity to make the highest exigencies worthy, and which deserves to be served, because it is worthy of the highest service." [42]

This aspect, which succeeds in giving content to God's holiness, was strictly the purpose of Isaiah's message. This involved, moreover, a change in man's religious outlook. Up to that time, what God seemed to require was the correct performance of cultic acts by which His sovereignty was recognized. Isaiah does not condemn the cult. But he shows that it is valueless, unless it is a sign of an inward attitude:

> *"To what purpose do you offer me the*
> *multitude of your sacrifices? . . .*
> *Take away the evil of your devices*
> *from my eyes."* [43]

If God is indeed not only the Almighty, but also the Holiest, if His transcendence is not only of the order of being, but also of that of goodness, what He asks from man is, first and foremost, that he should be holy, even as He is holy—*i.e.* God holds fast inwardly to His infinitely holy will, by fulfilling His commandments and observing His Law.

This point represents an essential stage in the revelation of God, one at which the connection appears between religion and morality. This connection may easily be misunderstood. There is a Pharisaism in the moral sphere, as there is a Pharisaism in worship. Nothing is further from the Bible than to reduce religion to morality. But it is the opposite that occurs here. Morality is integrated into religion inasmuch as duty, which is its sign, is shown to be based on the infinite holiness of the divine will which is imposed absolutely upon man. "The sense of moral duty," as Père de Montcheuil has rightly said, "is born when the motion issuing from the love of worthiness, which is God Himself, meets in ourselves an inward resistance. It interprets the statement that not only such resistance, but any resistance whatever, must be overcome." [44]

Indeed, as we have said, it seems impossible to reduce moral obligation to a social pressure or a law of personal development. If it were only this, it would not be needed—and it hardly seems to be needed today by those who label as "moral" the discipline which they manufacture for themselves. But such morality has no longer any connection with duty. The only thing with regard to which I am under a sense of duty is not that which I impose upon myself by constraint, but that to which I am unable to refuse the unconditional homage of my will. But nothing can be absolutely imposed on me except by a transcendent person. This is why moral duty can only be the veneration of the infinitely sacred will of God. The ultimate foundation of morality cannot be other than religious. Morality is worship by the will. And this is why sin is never anything but lack of love for God.

This is made clear in the basic text to which we must continually return when dealing with sanctity —the sixth chapter of *Isaiah*. The first reaction on the part of the Prophet, as he describes the approach of God's holiness, is a violent gesture of recoil. Contact with the infinite purity of the divine arouses in him an awareness of his own basic impurity, and therefore of his utter incompatibility with God:

*"Woe is me! because I have held my
    peace;
Because I am a man of unclean
    lips . . .
I have seen with my eyes the King of
    the Lord of hosts."* [45]

This is Peter's reaction too, at the time of the miraculous draught, when the divinity of Christ is revealed: "Depart from me, for I am a sinful man, O Lord." Thus we may say that the first sign of the approach of God's holiness within the soul is an increase of the sense of sin. There are saints who know what sin is, and sinners who do not. For if sin is only in practice a contempt for the will of God, only he who understands to what an extent that will is worthy to be loved, realizes the seriousness of sin.

But this first reaction, which causes sinful man to flee before the holiness of God, is followed by a second, which is the thirst for purification. For the soul cannot fail to love the awesome holiness of God without at the same time thirsting to be united with Him; and this contradiction is the very heart of genuine religion. But, to be united with Him, the soul must be purified, for only that which is holy can be one with the Holiest. So the soul turns towards the Holy Spirit, Who alone can work in her that fundamental purification which penetrates to the very root of her being.

This brings us to another characteristic of God's holiness. Insofar as He burns away all uncleanness, He appears as a consuming fire. This is shown in the sequel to our quotation from *Isaiah*: "And one of the seraphims flew to me, and in his hand was a live coal, which he had taken with the tongs from off the altar: and he touched my mouth, and said, behold, this hath touched thy lips; and thine iniquities shall be taken away: thy sin shall be cleansed." [46] What God burns away is not man's being, but his uncleanness. This brings us to the fact that if man fears as a danger the approach of the divine fire, this is not because he feels it to be a threat to his being, but because he feels he is threatened in his possessiveness, which is indeed the deepest level of his uncleanness.

Thus the holiness of God appears as a purifying fire to the sinful soul. But in that the fire purifies, the soul, freed from her bonds, feels an irresistible longing for that infinite beauty which tears her away from herself and from all things, in order to absorb her in itself. Otto describes this last aspect of holiness by the term *fascinatio*. The word expresses clearly the attraction that God exercises on the soul to whom His holiness is unveiled. This attraction is sovereign, insofar as it clears away all obstacles and breaks down all barriers. This is the folly of love that bursts forth in the soul of the saints. It appears as the last stage in the journey of the soul towards God, for it turns her utterly away from herself, in order that it may cause her to rest utterly in Him.

God is thus perceived first as an object of longing by the soul who seeks Him. Scripture often teaches us about the quest for God:

> "My soul hath desired thee in the
>   night;
> Yea, and with my spirit within me in
>   the morning early will I watch
>   to thee." [47]

This quest fills the works of the great mystics.
Thus St. Augustine describes the soul whom the
weight of love draws ever nearer to God; and
Gregory of Nyssa writes: "The soul, freed from
passions, flies forth, lightly and swiftly, from the
depths to the heights; and if nothing from below
interrupts her flight, the nature of the Good drawing to her those who contemplate her, she rises
ever higher above herself." [48] Thus the soul, as if
raised by supernatural gravitation, plunges ever on-
ward into the darkness of God.

    God shows Himself, then, as the repose of the
soul who finds 'Him and whose thirst He quenches.
"He that believeth in me shall never thirst," said
Christ to the Samaritan woman; and already the
Old Testament had described the joy that comes
from the possession of God:

> "How great is the goodness, O Lord,
> Which you have in store for those
>   who fear you." [49]

Excess of divine joy overwhelms the soul, beyond
all her powers of imagining. This is blessedness,
transcendent joy, and this joy blots out all other
joys. The mystics are never weary of describing
this total sufficiency of God to the soul who has

found the one thing needful. The Word of God, by touching the soul, awakens her to the experience of the divine realities in which she rejoices. "You have called me," exclaims St. Augustine, "you have cried, you have broken my deafness; you have blazed, you have cast forth sparks and broken my blindness; you have spread abroad a pleasant odor, and I have breathed it, and I pant after you; I have tasted, and I hunger and thirst after you. You have touched me, and you have burnt my soul with a holy longing for your peace." [50]

But these two aspects, in which God appears first as desirable and then as full of delight, are not two successive stages, so that having found God the soul no longer desires Him. God remains always beyond all that the soul can achieve. But by communing with the soul, He enlarges her capacity and makes her capable of fresh communion. Thus the soul is at the same time always overwhelmed with abundance and always thirsting after it. Mystical experience is at the same time, according to the profound view of Gregory of Nyssa, *stasis* and *kinêsis,* rest and movement. "And the soul that mounts up never pauses, going from beginnings to beginnings through beginnings which are without end." [51] The transcendence of God subsists in the very communication that He makes of Himself, in such a way that the beatific vision itself will be the eternal discovery of divine splendor beyond comparison, in which God will be at last known and yet never to be known, for ever known in perfection, yet never to be understood.

BIBLIOGRAPHY

P. Van Imschoot, *Théologie de l'Ancien Testament, I, Dieu,* 1954.

Jacques Guillet, *Thèmes bibliques,* 1950.

Andre Gelin, *Les ideés maîtresses de l'Ancien Testament,* 1946.

N. H. Snaith, *The Distinctive Ideas of the Old Testament,* 1944.

W. Eichrodt, *Theologie des Alten Testaments,* 1933-1935.

Andre Neher, *Amos,* 1949.

4

THE GOD OF
Jesus Christ

The Mosaic revelation, as compared with the cosmic revelation, represents a great advance in the knowledge of the true God; but it represents, nevertheless, nothing more than a stage. It is only in Jesus Christ that the hidden God is truly revealed: "No man hath seen God at any time: the only begotten Son, who is in the bosom of the Father, he hath declared him." [1] The *Epistle to the Hebrews* describes the sequence of revelations: "God, who, at sundry times and in divers manners spoke in times past to the fathers by the prophets, last of all, in these last hath spoken to us by his Son." [2] This revelation is that of the last days, after which there can be no further manifestations, for God has expressed His fullness in the Word.

The object of this revelation is the Trinity of Persons—that is, strictly speaking, the mystery of God, wholly inaccessible to human reason, hidden in darkness. All forms of knowledge and all comparisons that we bring to bear on this subject are deceiving, even those of the greatest theologians. They are only justified in the sight of reason insofar as they more or less clarify its apophatic nature, hidden as it is, and transcending all reason. For it will always remain true that the requirement of human reason, when it follows its inclination, is that of reducing everything to unity and seeing in all differences a secondary, subsidiary stage. This is so true that theologians like Eckhardt have tended to see in the Trinity a manifestation of primordial, unfathomable unity. But in reality the paradox is that the Three is as primitive as the One. It participates in the structure of absolute Being. Without doubt the master-key to Christian theology, which distinguishes it utterly from all rational theodicy, is contained in the statement that the Trinity of Persons constitutes the structure of Being, and that love is therefore as primary as existence.

At the same time, this inaccessible mystery is the whole of Christianity—not merely a single aspect, but its very essence. For Christianity is the appeal addressed to man by the Father, inviting him to share in the life of the Son through the gift of the Spirit. This constitutes the very essence of Christianity. The first word that a child hears the Church speak over him is: "I baptize thee in the Name of the Father, and of the Son, and of the Holy Ghost." He is thrown, as a creature of flesh and blood, into the abyss of Trinitarian life, to which all life and all eternity will have no other object than to accustom him. It is in the gift that It makes of Its own life that the Trinity at the same time communicates and reveals Itself, estranging man from his own ways and views in order to transfer him into Itself.

Thus it remains true of this supreme revelation of God that, as we said of the preceding revelations, it is through His action in the world and in man that God makes Himself known. Here again, Scripture confronts us with facts; and it is on these facts that theology is to reflect. But while the Old Testament showed us God the One making a covenant with Israel and drawing it away from idols, the New Testament confronts us with God the Three revealed in Jesus Christ. This progressive revelation corresponds to a course of divine instruction, whose development Gregory of Nazianzen has well described: "The Old Testament has clearly, though darkly, revealed the Father and the Son. The New Testament has revealed the Son and provided a glimpse of the divinity of the Holy Ghost. Now the Holy Ghost dwells among us and is revealed more clearly." [3] It was first necessary that faith in the unity of God, in monotheism, should be profoundly rooted in a human race always inclined towards polytheism, in order that, at the heart of that unity, the Trinity of Persons could be revealed without any danger. This revelation of the oneness of God fills the Old Testament to overflowing. The New Testament reveals chiefly the divinity of the Word. According to the excellent view of Gregory, the revelation of the Holy Ghost fills the Time of the Church, which is the manifestation of Its mighty works.

Gregory of Nazianzen continues by saying: "It was necessary to proceed by successive perfectings, by 'degrees', in David's phrase; it was necessary to advance from radiance to radiance, through ever more luminous movements of advance, in order that the light of the Trinity might finally be seen to shine forth." The brightness of the Trinity is such that man's sight could not have borne it. According to the ancient view of Irenaeus, it was necessary that God should acclimatize man gradually to the vision of His unendurable glory. The light that blazes from the countenance of the Father is already too overwhelming a sight for men of flesh and blood. It is by gradual stages that the divinity of the Word appears darkly in the Old Testament, and clearly in the Gospel. The Holy Spirit in Its turn crowns the education of mankind with the Trinitarian vision. Thus man goes on from glory to glory, and the whole history of salvation may be considered as a gradual unveiling of the ineffable Trinity.

But if the New Testament alone gives us knowledge of the Three Persons, at the same time it throws light upon the wholeness of God's plan, and displays it as being entirely the work of the Trinity. It appears, in fact, to be a history of the divine missions; all the works of God are fulfilled by the Three Persons, but each acts in a particular manner. St. Irenaeus explains this clearly when he writes: "The Father is well pleased and commands, the Son works and creates, the Spirit nourishes and gives increase, and man moves little by little towards perfection." [4] The Father is He who sends, the Word and the Spirit are sent. Thus the divine missions are like a reflection of the eternal relationships between the Persons; their economy appears as theology, and it is through this epiphany of the Trinitarian life that man glimpses something of Its eternal existence.

So again we follow the very order of revelation, when we begin our account of the Trinity of Persons with Their action in the world. The New Testament is in fact essentially a testimony borne to this action; it shows us Christ, Who is God, and Who is distinct from the Father; it shows us the Spirit, Who is God since He bestows the life of God, and Who is sent by the Father and the Son. It is through the divine works carried out by the Three Persons that theology is to discover little by little, in an endless task of contemplation, what They are in Themselves. That is why in this chapter we shall speak of the Trinity as revealed in Scripture—*i.e.* above all as a series of missions. Later we shall develop theologically the mystery of Their relationship. Before speaking in particular of the Word and the Spirit, we shall speak of these missions in general.

They begin, we said, with creation. All is the work of the Three Persons. St. John says of the Word: "All things were made by him," [5] and the *Epistle to the Hebrews,* in the sequel to the passage we quoted above, declares that God "in these days hath spoken to us by his Son, whom he hath appointed heir of all things." [6] Against the Gnostics, who contrasted the God of creation with the God of redemption, St. Irenaeus insists on the unity of God's plan. Christ is that same Word of God who created the world and man in the beginning, and Who, in the fullness of time, came down to earth to reawaken His creature, to restore him and grant him incorruptibility.

We have already had occasion to encounter the theme of creation, both in relation to cosmic religion and to Mosaic revelation. But each of these revelations shows us new wonders. On the level of cosmic religion, the theme appeared as a sign of the fundamental distinction between God and the creature, and of the creature's subsistence in his basic dependence on God. On the level of Mosaic revelation, we encountered the theme as the first phase in the history of salvation, of God's plan which began with time (since it is time itself), but whose content remained veiled. From the beginning, the Three Persons created in Their own image a human being, called to share in Their life and to be led by Them into Paradise.

Thus the light of the New Testament comes to illuminate, retrospectively, the Old. In Origen's phrase, it "whitens the fields of the Scriptures for the harvest," [7] by bringing forth what was only a seed. In the beginning, says St. Irenaeus, the gift of the Spirit was still tentative, for the hand of God, which is the Word, had not yet grasped man in that everlasting grip which was to be known one day as the Incarnation. But meanwhile these beginnings of mankind were bathed in a supernatural light, and the artists of the Middle Ages were right to show us Adam and Eve talking with the Three Persons. Since man appeared, formed by the Three Persons, He has been called to share in Their life. Paradise is the place where the divine energy is at work, and where that tree of life is to be found which communicates incorruptibility. In all this there is a foreshadowing of the Church.

This is expressed by the Fathers of the Church in the doctrine of "man created in the image and likeness of God." Faithful to the literal meaning of the biblical text, Athanasius and Gregory of Nyssa do not see in the image and likeness two different realities, but two aspects of the same reality.[8] For them, this reality is not reason, which is simply nature, but that sharing in the life of the Trinity which is grace. Made in the image of the only begotten Son, who is the perfect image of the Father, the first Adam is already called in the Son to be the child of the Father and the temple of the Spirit. Thus the creation of man appears, in the light of the New Testament, to be already plunged in the sphere of Trinitarian grace.

The history of God's people, Israel, in its turn sheds fresh light on the subject, for it becomes the place of the *magnalia* of the Trinity. For if it is the shape of God's total plan that it should be through the Word and the Spirit that the Father should accomplish His mysterious designs, this was also true in the time of the Old Covenant. St. Paul already states this when he shows us in the desert rock, from which a stream arises, a foretelling of Christ—*i.e.* an act of the Word in the history of the world. St. Irenaeus is faithful to this spirit when he sees in the history of Israel the action of the Word and the Holy Ghost, by Whom man was created, and Who acclimatize him gradually to the life of the Trinity in order to prepare him for that inwardness of human and divine nature which is to be fulfilled in due time in the Incarnation. In this way the Fathers of the Church acknowledged the theophanies of the Old Testament as revelations of the Word.

No one has expressed this view more profoundly than St. Irenaeus. "All the visions of the Old Testament," he writes, "represent the Son of God speaking with men and living in their midst. He did not leave the human race, but remained with them, foretelling what must happen and teaching men the things of God. Thus He foreshadowed in our terms, and showed us through imagery, what was to come." [9] So, like creation, the Covenant shines, in the light of the Old Testament, with the brightness of the Trinity. We said that the Covenant foreshadowed the Incarnation, insofar as it was a sign of a God who comes to meet man and establish with him a living kinship. But now, to be more accurate, it is the Word of God who, according to Irenaeus, foreshadows His Incarnation by making Himself familiar with the ways of men.

This familiarizing of the Word of God with the ways of men prepares for the Incarnation, insofar as the latter is a movement of God towards man. But Irenaeus notices, too, another aspect: the

Word of God at the same time familiarizes man with the things of God, in order to make him fit to enter, through the Incarnation, into full communion with Him: "God created man from the beginning, because of His munificence; He chose the patriarchs for their salvation; He educated His restless people, by teaching them to serve God; He sent His prophets into the world, accustoming man to bear His Spirit and live in communion with God." [10] And later Irenaeus says: "Thus the Word of God, traversing all times, educated His people, calling them through secondary things to primary things, through imagery to reality, through things temporal to things eternal, through the carnal to the spiritual." [11]

But only the light of Christianity enables us to see in the Old Testament this manifestation of the Trinity, whereas it is the very subject-matter of the New Testament, whose purpose is to bear witness to the Incarnation of the Word and the outpouring of the Spirit, and which through these two missions teaches us to distinguish Them from the Father. All these mysteries of Christ appear as the work of the Three Persons. St. Luke shows us the Holy Spirit descending on Mary to arouse in her the humanity of Christ, and St. John shows us the Word of God becoming "flesh," *i.e.* taking human nature. It is the Spirit who leads Zachariah to the Temple and Jesus to the desert. It is He whom the Incarnate Word, present in Mary, shows forth in John the Baptist at the Visitation. Above all, the Three Persons appear in the great Theophany of the Baptism, when the Voice of the Father bears witness that Christ, who plunges in the waters of Jordan, is His beloved Son, while the Spirit descends upon Him in the likeness of a dove. On two further occasions, the Voice of the Father is to bear witness to Christ—at two solemn moments, that of the Transfiguration, and that of the Agony, according to St. John.[12]

This revelation, which remains veiled in the Synoptics, appears in all its fullness in St. John's Gospel. The only begotten Son, distinct from the Father, shares completely in His divine nature: "I and the Father are one." The work of salvation is the joint work of the Father and the Son: "For the Father loveth the Son, and sheweth him all things which himself doeth."[13] The Son is sent by the Father. He fulfils the work that the Father has given Him. His mission is to make known the Father and communicate His life. But, as He does nothing save with the Father, he who sees Him sees the Father, and he who believes in Him has eternal life. Thus, through the mission of the Word, the Trinity of Persons is revealed at the same time as Their unity; eternal life, which is the life of God, draws near to man through Him, to take hold of man and awaken him.

For this work of redemption is not only Threefold insofar as it leads mankind, through the mediation of Jesus, to share in the life of the Three Persons. It is the mystery of filial adoption that is the boundary of the divine work, that design hidden in God which St. Paul describes: "Blessed be the God and Father of our Lord Jesus Christ, who hath . . . chosen us in him before the foundation of the world, that we should be holy and unspotted in his sight in charity: hath predestinated us unto the adoption of children by Jesus Christ to himself, according to the purpose of his will, unto the praise of the glory of his grace." [14] This adoption as children, accomplished in substance by the Incarnation of the Word, is conveyed by the gift of the Spirit, which is "the spirit of adoption of sons, whereby we cry, Abba (Father)." [15]

This outpouring of the Spirit is granted in baptism. The Time of the Church continues to be that of the great works of the Trinity. These are the sacraments which are strictly divine works, effecting a divine life in man. Thus in the Time of the Church the Trinity continues to be revealed through Its works. Baptism, as St. Paul has shown, conforms man to the death and resurrection of Christ. [16] Thus He conveys spiritual life to man through the gift of the Spirit; and man is led through Baptism to intimate contact with the Father, in the freedom of the sons of God. Thus to be a Christian is to be born into the life of the Trinity, which is the incorruptible life of God, possessed by the Three Persons and conveyed by Them in a pattern of incomprehensible love.

None has described better than St. Irenaeus this birth in the Trinity: "When we are born again through baptism in the Name of the Three Persons, we are enriched, by a second birth, with the good things that are in God the Father, by means of His Son, with the Holy Ghost. Those who are baptized receive the Spirit of God, who gives them to the Word, that is, the Son; and the Son takes them and offers them to the Father, and the Father grants them incorruptibility. Therefore without the Holy Ghost we cannot see the Word of God, and without the Son no one can come to the Father; since the knowledge of the Father is the Son, and the knowledge of the Son of God is gained by means of the Holy Ghost; but it is the Son whose function it is to distribute the Holy Ghost, according to the good pleasure of the Father, to those whom the Father chooses and in the way that the Father chooses." [17]

But all this is a mystery which is wholly spiritual and forbidden to carnal man. Only the Holy Ghost gives us understanding of it. Carnal man has no means of grasping it by himself. This is why it remains alien to him, since it is in truth alien to him; yet the reality of the Trinity is revealed through this very strangeness. It is the hidden life of the transcendent God; and if it became accessible to carnal man it would not be one and the same. In conveying it to man, the Trinity remains a mystery. It is not to man that It adapts Itself; it is man whom It raises above himself and adapts to Itself. This is why the Christian life, which is the life of the Trinity, is itself an incomprehensible mystery and a stumbling-block to those who see it from outside. The darkness that conceals the Trinity from profane sight also

conceals from it the mysterious acts of the Trinity
in the soul of the saints.

Just as it is through the Covenant that the ways
of the living God are revealed to us, and that He
appears to us as justice, truth and love, so it is
through adoption that the Persons are revealed to
us as Father, Son and Spirit. These are the prop-
erties of the Persons, of which we must now
speak. We shall do this by turning first to the testimony of Scripture, in which each of the Persons
is revealed through the pattern of salvation. Only
later shall we be able, by reflecting on the facts as
given there, to understand something of the eternal
relationships between the Persons. I shall chiefly
emphasize the Word and the Spirit, the understanding of which is vital to the New Testament.

The first revelation is that of the Father. He is
the principle, the origin, the *archè* of the Trinity.
Thus in creation, which is the joint work of the
Three, like all Their works *ad extra,* the Father
reveals Himself in a special manner. It is He who
proffers the creative Word: "God said, Let there
be light." And it is He who is well pleased when
He surveys the accomplished work: "God saw that
it was good." Here Gregory of Nazianzen is right
in saying that the Old Testament is a revelation of
the Father, although, strictly speaking, it is the
revelation of the One God, and everything in it is
the joint work of the Three Persons. But insofar
as it is a question of origination, of the origin of

creation, the origin of election, the origin of mission, the Old Testament refers especially to Him.

It shows Him to us also as the Father. This fatherhood with regard to creation seems to be a reflection, in the order of mission, of the eternal relationships. Thus when Christ speaks of "your Father which is in heaven: for he maketh his sun to rise up upon the good and bad and raineth upon the just and unjust," [18] He is not speaking of the Father in the eternal relationship which He has with His only begotten Son, but in the paternal Providence which is the continuation of creation. Similarly, when Osee says of God: "Because Israel was a child, and I loved him; and I called my son out of Egypt," (11 : 1) he refers, as we have seen, to the relationship created by election and the covenant between Yahweh and Israel, which is a visible theophany of His Fatherhood in relation to His own begotten Son.

Thus the Person of the Father appears in the Old Testament in the reflection of His creative, providential action. But it will only be fully revealed in the New Testament, for it cannot openly appear except in relation to the Son, whom only the New Testament reveals in His personal reality. But even so, it is not at first revealed directly, but in relation to the Son in His Incarnation. So again it is through the redemptive pattern that the Fatherhood is revealed. It is through the works He accomplishes that Christ appears in relation to His Father, when He is singled out for approval at the Baptism, when He beseeches Him to let the cup pass at the Passion, when He commends His Spirit into the Father's hands. The Trinity appears here in the mirror of the divine economy.

This becomes still clearer in the Second Person. The Old Testament reveals Him darkly as the Word of the Father. The phrase here must again be carefully interpreted. The Hebrew *dabar,* which the Greek translates as *logos* and the Latin as *verbum,* has a well-defined content. For the Greeks, the *logos* is chiefly the *word* as intelligibly enunciated; this is how the expression comes to mean the inward law of things, their reason. But the Hebrew *dabar* has quite another meaning, as Gerhard Kittel has noted.[19] The *word* appears here as performing what it enunciates, as the speech of blessing or cursing. It is an act, not merely a meaning.

Applied to the divine sphere, the Word of God is revealed, above all, as a force. It is, first of all, a creative force. "By the words of the Lord are his works," says the son of Sirach.[20] St. John too, proclaiming the identity of the creative Word with that of the Incarnate Word, says: "All things were made by him." The efficacy of the Word of God is clearly shown in *Isaias:*

> *And as the rain and the snows come*
> *down from heaven*
> *And return no more thither,*
> *But soak the earth and water it, and*
> *make it to spring*
> *And give seed to the sower, and*
> *bread to the eater:*

> *So shall my word be, which shall go*
> *forth from my mouth,*
> *But it shall do whatsoever I please*
> *. . ."* [21]

It is this creative Word, by whom all was made, and by whom every moment of time is provided, that St. John, by a foreshortening which throws into relief the staggering paradox of Christianity, shows to be none other than Jesus of Nazareth: "And the Word was made flesh." For it is in fact the same Word on whose pattern the Father made man in the beginning, who, according to St. Irenaeus, came to touch again this *plasma* which was His (though it had strayed far from Him), and to restore it in Himself in a conclusive manner.

But the work of the Word is not only that of creation. He is also the Word who judges, the sharp sword that divides, that saves and condemns. Thus the *Book of Wisdom* shows Him to us:

> *"For while all things were in quiet*
> *silence,*
> *And the night was in the midst of her*
> *course.*
> *The almighty word leapt down from*
> *heaven . . .*
> *With a sharp sword carrying thy un-*
> *feigned commandment . . ."* [22]

The Roman liturgy applies this text to the Incarnation of the Word in the introit to the Mass for Sunday in the Octave of Christmas; and Tauler comments on the eternal generation of the Word in the soul of the saints. St. John likewise applies this theme to the Incarnate Word:

"And I saw heaven opened, and behold a white horse; and he that sat upon him was called faithful and true, and with justice doth he judge and make war. And he was clothed with a garment sprinkled with blood; and his name is called *The Word of God* . . . And out of his mouth proceedeth a sharp two-edged sword." [23] The *Epistle to the Hebrews* cries in its turn: "For the Word of God is living, and effectual, and more piercing than any two-edged sword, and reaching unto the division of the soul and the spirit." [24]

Finally, the Word of God is a revealing Word. It is to this that the *Book of Samuel* (I Kings) refers when it tells us that the child Samuel did not recognize Him, because "the word of the Lord was precious in those days; there was no manifest vision." [25] It is this Word that is delivered to the Prophets, and is the principle, as we have said, by which the revelation comes to them. But this revelation that is made to men is only a created reflection of that eternal manifestation by which the Father proffers the eternal Word, who is His perfect image, in whom He acknowledges His whole presence, and in whom He rejoices infinitely. Through the mission of the Word, it is eternal generation that is revealed.

If St. John shows us in the Second Person the creative illuminative Word, St. Paul prefers to describe Him as subsistent wisdom. Here again it is by reference to the Old Testament that the Second

Person is characterized. Wisdom, *hohkma,* which the Greeks translated as *sophia,* meant, for the peoples of the East, prudence in the conduct of life, such as they found in the sayings of wise men. Thus the princes of Oriental monarchies compiled Books of Wisdom for the education of their subjects. When Solomon made Israel a great monarchy in the Oriental style, he wished likewise to endow his people with a monument of sagacity. "Soloman also spoke three thousand parables: and his poems were a thousand and five," as we are told in the *Book of Kings.*[26] For this reason the Bible puts his name to the Books of *Proverbs* and *Wisdom.*

But the idea of "wisdom" takes on a new character when it is transplanted into Yahwist religion. It is no longer simply human prudence, but the conduct of life according to the ways of Yahweh. For Israel, the sole rule governing man's existence is the Law of God revealed to Moses and the Prophets. Wisdom is thus identified with the Torah, the Law, and it comes to mean, not merely the Law of God, such as existed in His communication with man, but the very Thought of God, the underlying Archetype of that Law. Thus it is Wisdom that presides over the whole divine scheme; in Wisdom God has formed the plan of His mighty works, and in Wisdom He watches over their completion.

The Wisdom literature devotes some noble passages to the praise of this aspect of divinity. *Proverbs* contains this description:

"The Lord begot me, the firstborn of
    his ways,
the forerunner of his prodigies of
    long ago;
From of old I was poured forth,
at the first, before the earth . . .
Before the mountains were settled
    into place,
before the hills, I was brought forth
    . . .
Then was I beside him as his crafts-
    man
and I was his delight day by day,
Playing before him all the while,
playing on the surface of the earth
and I found delight in the sons of
    men." [27]

Wisdom presides over God's creation, but precedes
it, being founded from eternity. This is one of the
texts that are most often quoted by subsequent theologians.

Wisdom is described in turn by the *Book of
Wisdom* as presiding not only over creation, but
also over the destiny of God's people. It shows Wisdom saving Noah at the time of the Flood, and
Lot at the destruction of Sodom. It is Wisdom who
leads Joseph "in the right way" and delivers Israel
from the Egyptian captivity. Here we find the
sources of Irenaeus' conception of the function of the
Word in the history of salvation. Through these
manifestations Wisdom reveals her essence:

> *"For she is a breath of the power*
> *"For she is an aura of the might of*
>   *God*
> *and a pure effusion of the glory of the*
>   *Almighty;*
> *therefore nought that is sullied enters*
>   *into her.*
> *For she is the refulgence of eternal*
>   *light,*
> *the spotless mirror of the power of*
>   *God,*
> *the image of his goodness . . .*
> *Indeed, she reaches from end to end*
>   *mightily*
> *and governs all things well."* [28]

Thus Wisdom appears in her eternal reality as the perfect image of God, as the complete expression of His infinite perfection.

Moreover, it is with this language that St. Paul and the whole tradition after him describe the Second Person. In Jesus there is revealed the subsistent personal reality of that Wisdom which the Old Testament described in her manifestations, though without showing them as subsistent. Thus, at the outset of the *Epistle to the Colossians,* Paul writes of the Son, "who is the image (*eikôn*) of the invisible God, the firstborn of every creature. For in him were all things created in heaven and on earth." [29] So, too, the author of the *Epistle to the Hebrews,* inspired by St. Paul, in a text which is the leit-motif of our present chapter, applies to the Second Person the language of *Wisdom:*

> *"God, who, at sundry times and in divers manners, spoke in times past to the fathers by the prophets, last of all, In these days hath spoken to us by his Son, whom he hath appointed heir of all things, by whom also he made the world . . . Who being the brightness of his glory, and the figure of his substance and upholding all things by the word of his power, making purgation of sins, sitteth on the right hand of the majesty on high."* [30]

Here is expressed the whole basic theology of the Word, such as the New Testament itself inaugurates. The Apostles were confronted with the fact of Christ, who claimed divine authority and power. This was the basic, elemental, fundamental datum of Revelation. When they sought for language in which to express this fact, the Apostles turned to the Old Testament, and borrowed their terminology from it. That is why this basic theology is an entirely biblical theology, showing the presence, in the Person of Christ, of that Wisdom of which the Old Testament only provided glimpses, but which is revealed in the New Testament in all its personal subsistence.

However, the term that brings us deepest into the understanding of the Second Person is that of "the Son"—an expression frequently used in the Old Testament in various senses. But its use in the New Testament, and especially by Christ Himself, proves, as Vincent Taylor says, that it belongs to the knowledge that Jesus had of Himself, that He was in a special sense the Son of God.[31] The first text in which the word appears makes this clear. It comes from *Matthew:* "All things are delivered to me by my Father: and no man knoweth the Son, but the Father; neither doth anyone know the Father, but the Son, and he to whom it shall please the Son to reveal him." [32] It is clear from this that there is between the Son and the Father a unique relationship, that they belong to the same sphere of existence, that there is complete mutual contact between them.

This is the theology of the Son that pervades the *Gospel According to St. John,* while that of the Word appears only in the Prologue. The Son comes from the Father: "I came forth from the Father, and am come into the world." [33] He belongs to the same order of existence as the Father. He alone knows the Father, and this is why He alone can make Him known. He is the object of the Father's love, and this love is concentrated in Him. He is the Son in whom the Father is well pleased. He has one thought and one will with the Father: "The Son cannot do anything of himself, but what he seeth the Father doing." [34] His likeness to the Father is such that he who has seen Him has seen the Father. Between the Father and Him there is mutual immanence: "Thou, Father, in me, and I in thee." [35] Thus, according to St. John, the relations between the Father and the Son in the order of the divine economy make transparently clear the perfect unity of Their divine Nature and the perfect distinction between Their Persons. Never will human eyes penetrate more deeply into the innermost relationship between the Father and the Son than did those of the Apostle who lay upon Jesus' breast.

The revelation of the Spirit presents a similar development, with the addition, as Gregory of Nazianzen well understood, that the Gospels are only a small part of the Spirit's activity, and that this activity is set forth in the Time of the Church, beginning at Pentecost. The Hebrew word which the Greek has translated *pneuma* is *ruah*. More than anywhere else, we must be careful here to find the exact meaning; for the word *esprit* is susceptible of a multitude of ambiguities which give entirely distinct meanings, as we shall see first in a frequent image, that of breath. The Greeks preserved here the idea of a subtle form of matter; thus it serves to describe the non-material element in man, the soul as contrasted with the body. Such is the familiar philosophical contrast.[36]

But for the Hebrews *ruah* means a breath of wind as it appears in the storm. The ideas connected with it are not those of non-materiality, but of power, of irresistible force. Consequently the idea of *esprit,* applied to God, does not mean His non-materiality, but His irresistible power, by which He accomplishes His mighty works. Thus in the scene at Pentecost, the outpouring of the Spirit is accompanied by a shaking of the whole house. Applied to man, it refers to that in him which is the work of God's power. Thus the Pauline contrast between spirit and flesh does not by any means cover that of soul and body. It is the contrast between the whole man, soul and body, when it is enlivened by divine energy, and the whole man, soul and body, when it is abandoned to its own misery. It is thus that for St. Paul there are spiritual bodies and carnal spirits, which would be a contradiction if body were contrasted with spirit.

We see how many false problems may be resolved in this way. Christians are often accused of despising the body, and it is true that we often encounter this depreciation; but this error is due to substituting Platonic opposites for Christian opposites. This can be a source of grave errors in spirituality. Similarly, Christians may give the impression that they are on the side of the world of intellect against that of matter. Again, even the word "spirituality" is ambiguous. When we speak of "Eastern spirituality," we speak of the possession of its true inwardness; when we speak of Christian spirituality, we speak of the supernatural works of the Holy Spirit in the soul.

It is first of all in the order of creation that the activity of the Spirit is revealed. It is the *Creator Spiritus;* and indeed it makes its first appearance in verse 2 of *Genesis:* "The spirit (*ruah*) of God was stirring above the waters." The image is that of the eagle beating the air above its nest to make the egrets fly. So the Spirit of God arouses creation from nothingness. This theme appears again and again in the Old Testament:

> *"If he were to take back his spirit to*
> *himself,*
> *withdraw to himself his breath,*
> *All flesh would perish together,*
> *and man would return to the dust."* [37]

The liturgy takes this up, applying it justly to the cosmos renewed by grace, in the verse which the *Psalms* apply to the first creation:

> *"When you send forth your spirit,*
> *they are created,*
> *and you renew the face of the earth."* [38]

The action of the Spirit is later revealed in history. It is to be exercised in two ways: first it is the Spirit of Yahweh who seizes upon certain people to arouse them by superhuman power to the accomplishment of certain great works of God. This appears especially in the *Book of Judges*, which refers to the conquest of Canaan. "The Spirit of the Lord enveloped Gedeon, and he blew the horn" (*Judges*, 34:14); thus he aroused the courage of the troops and led them to victory. It was the same Spirit that "came mightily upon" Samson, giving him strength to rend a young lion with his bare hands, and to slay thirty men single-handed (*Judges*, 14: 6-19), to break, "as flax that is consumed by fire," the new cords that bound his arms, and then, armed with the jawbone of an ass, to slay a thousand Philistines (15: 14-15).

Elsewhere the Spirit gives certain men knowledge of God's plan. We say in the Creed: "Who spake by the prophets." The Prophet is he to whom the Holy Spirit shows the secret of His ways. It is the Holy Spirit alone who fathoms the depths of God and shows us His mystery. In other words, the Holy Spirit leads history through His anointed, and explains it through His prophets; but it is He who is here the primal cause. We should have to quote all the Prophets at this point. Thus David: "The Spirit of the Lord hath spoken by me, and his word by my tongue" (2 *Sam.* [2 Kings] 23:2). Thus Ezekiel: "The spirit entered into me . . . and set me upon my feet: and I heard him speaking to me" (*Ezek.*, 2:2). The *Second Epistle of Peter* recalls this doctrine: "Holy men of God spoke, inspired by the Holy Ghost" (1:21).

Pagan antiquity also had a doctrine of prophecy and divination, but among the Ancients divination was based on another phenomenon; it was connected with the idea of *pneuma;* but it is a question here of a material breath, emanating from the earth, which in trances enters into the diviner, puts him in relation with unknown cosmic forces, and enables him to perceive connections that escape ordinary consciousness. Verbeke gives a useful account of this process: "The power to predict coming events is allied to universal sympathy, to the interdependence of cosmic events; all the happenings of the cosmos are elements in a great whole, among which there is continual interaction. However, all men are not able to discover these secret connections. Yet there are certain privileged men who can attain divinatory enthusiasm." [39] We see here the difference between the two conceptions: for pagan thought, it is a matter of hidden energies in the cosmos which must be tapped; in the biblical perspective the action of *ruah* raises man above his nature, bringing him into the world of God.

This action of the Spirit, which directs sacred history, is to appear in all its fullness in the third stage of the *magnalia* of God, that of the Incarnation. It is the Holy Spirit that is the agent here. The archangel Gabriel says to Mary: "The Holy Ghost shall come upon thee, and the power of the most High shall overshadow thee" [40]; and in *Matthew:* "Before they came together, she was found with child, of the Holy Ghost." [41] At the Baptism, the Holy Spirit descends upon Jesus in the form of a dove, to inaugurate His public life and His prophetic ministry: "And Jesus, being full of the Holy Ghost, returned from the Jordan, and was led by the Spirit into the desert." [42] Jesus applies to Himself the words of *Isaias:* "The Spirit of the Lord . . . hath anointed me," [43] and "I cast out devils by the Spirit of God." [44]

Thus the Incarnation opened a new age in the history of the world, that in which the Holy Spirit was plenteously spread abroad through the manhood of Jesus. After the Ascension, the Spirit that was in Him was communicated to the Church, which is His Body. This outpouring of the Spirit took place on the day of Pentecost: "And suddenly there came a sound from heaven, as of a mighty wind coming, and it filled the whole house where they were sitting . . . And they were all filled with the Holy Ghost, and they began to speak with divers tongues." [45] The result of this descent of the Spirit is twofold. On the one hand, it aroused the Apostles, those weak men who had been scattered on Good Friday, with a new, superhuman power. They went forth now to bear witness, to perform the great acts of God. There came upon them a divine power whereby they spoke with authority, and with an effect beyond that of human words; they performed miracles, they converted hearts.

But all these facts which continue the action of the Spirit in the Old Testament only translate this action in an outward manner; for the new event of Pentecost is the coming of the Spirit into souls, to communicate to them the new life, that of grace. As the Spirit at the beginning brooded upon the waters, arousing in them biological life, so now the Holy Spirit performs a new act of creation, that of the *spiritual* life in the strict sense of the word. This life is superior to the forces of nature and intellect, for it shares in the life of God Himself. The chief text here is that of the *Epistle to the Romans:* "You have received the Spirit of adoption of sons, whereby we cry, Abba (Father)." [46] Only the Holy Spirit can permit us to know in faith "the deep things of God." [47]

In this new activity, which is that of the creation of the cosmos of grace, the Holy Spirit is revealed with greater clarity. First it appears as divine; it is the *Holy* Spirit, *i.e.* its function is, strictly speaking, the divinization of the soul; it brings us into the sphere of God, and that is the whole purpose of Christianity. Already, from the beginning, it has appeared to us as performing works beyond the power of man. But here it appears as performing a work which is strictly holy and divinizing. Henceforth, the nature of *ruah* is revealed in this way. It is truly a divine force working in history to achieve the transfiguration of the world and the edification of the Body of Christ. The Spirit is the living, working soul of the Church, edifying the mystical Christ through the centuries.

But a further aspect, of hidden origin, now makes its appearance: this is the personal character of the Spirit. It is not only a question of an impersonal power, as the Old Testament might lead us to suppose. Christ presents the Spirit as a new Intercessor and puts it on the same level as Himself—and His own personality is beyond question. The *Acts* attribute to it personal activity; it bears witness, it teaches, it feels sorrow at unfaithfulness, it dwells in the soul; it is thus a personal presence, a presence more intimately concerned with man than the general presence of God in creation, and even connected with the nature of grace. We are the *temple of the Holy Spirit,* says St. Paul (1 *Cor.,* 3:16). Thus man is fully entitled to pray:

Veni Creator Spiritus,
Mentes tuorum visita.

We began by discussing the activity of the Holy Spirit in the life of the cosmos; then we saw how it operated in history, and finally in the world of grace. In this way it is revealed in all its reality, as God and as a Person. But elsewhere we have seen that the Word was also revealed to us as God and as a Person. Before Them, the Father appeared to us as the original Principle, He also being both God and a Person. Thus, little by little, the mystery has been unveiled before us of a God in whom there are Three Persons. This result is obtained by studying the evidence presented by the facts recorded in the Old and New Testaments.

But now comes the final question—that of the relationships between these Persons. For we see that, before They are revealed in nature and history, They exist eternally in God. Therefore there must be eternal relationships between them. These relationships are to be seen reflected in the mirror of the missions of the Trinity. It will be the task of theologians—and St. John is their leader—to begin with the biblical data that have an essential bearing on the activity of the Three Persons in time, and to try to contemplate and express their eternal relationships. Thus theology will rise towards primordial reality, shrouded in darkness and forbidden to human sight, but accessible to man's understanding through its activity in the world.

The life of the Trinity is a perfect unity. The Father, the Son, and the Spirit are but a single God. "I and the Father are one," says Christ in *St. John* (10:30). This implies the joint possession of the same single divine nature: "All things whatsoever the Father hath, are mine" (16:15). For "the Father loveth the Son, and sheweth him all things which himself doth"

(5:20). He communicates to the Son the life that is His: "For as the Father hath life in himself; so he hath given to the Son also to have life in himself" (5:26). And as He has the power of judgment, He "hath given him power to do judgment" (5:27). Thus Christ can say of the Father: "All my things are thine, and thine are mine" (17:10). This perfect unity is the pattern and source of all unity: "That they may be one, as we also are one" (17:22).

However, this union is not the communication by the Father of a life which He first possessed alone. As Père Lebreton has written, St. John insists on the eternal character of this union and on the perfect mutuality which it implies. He expresses this through the doctrine of the immanence of the divine Persons in one another, which implies their eternal co-existence: "I am in the Father and the Father in me" (*John*, 14:10). And Christ continues: "The words that I speak to you I speak not of myself. But the Father who abideth in me, he doth the works. Believe you not that I am in the Father, and the Father in me?" (*John*, 14:10-11). This mutual immanence of the Persons is the seal of their coeternity. It constitutes the insurmountable barrier between the doctrine of the Trinity and any philosophy of emenation. It makes the Trinity of Persons constitute the very being of God, and not a secondary feature in the unity of nature.

It follows from this that the Son was perfectly with the Father; he who knows Him knows the

Father in Him in His perfect likeness, since there is nothing that distinguishes the Father except the being of the Son. This is the meaning of Christ's reply to Philip, who asked Him: "Lord, shew us the Father, and it is enough for us." Christ replies: "Have I been so long a time with you; and have you not known me, Philip? he that seeth me seeth the Father also" (*John*, 14: 8-9). Accordingly, he that honors the Father honors the Son also (*John*, 5:23). Conversely, the Jews reject Christ "because they have not known the Father, nor me" (*John*, 16:3). "He who honoreth not the Son honoreth not the Father" (*John*, 5:23); and "what things soever he doth, these the Son also doth in like manner" (*John*, 5:19).

But this unique Godhead, the object of a unique worship, is possessed by each Person according to His distinguishing property. This mode of possession is what formally constitutes Him as a Person, since this alone is proper to Him. The Son is He who is begotten by the Father. Throughout St. John's Gospel, this generation is expressed by the dependence of the Son in relation to the Father, which implies no inferiority, but only a certain order: "Amen, amen, I say unto you, The Son cannot do anything of himself, but what he seeth the Father doing: for what things soever he doth, these the Son doth in like manner" (*John*, 5:19). As Père Lebreton again points out, it is not a question here of the human actions of Christ, but of His eternal, divine activity.[48] Similarly this eternal pre-existence of the Word "in the beginning with God" was stated in the *Prologue*. St. John returns to this theme in his *Gospel*, when he reports Christ as speaking of "the glory which I had, before the world was, with thee" (*John*, 17:5).

Just as the Son is the One God with the Father, so is He with the Spirit. As the Son perfectly knows the Father, so "the things also that are of God no man knoweth, but the Spirit of God . . . for the Spirit searcheth all things, yea, the deep things of God" (1 *Cor.*, 2: 10-11). But its own character is that it possesses this fullness of the divine Being by receiving it both from the Father and the Son. On the one hand, St. John tells us that the Spirit "proceedeth from the Father" (15:26) and is "the Comforter, which is the Holy Ghost, whom the Father will send in my name" (14:26). But elsewhere St. John shows us the Spirit as a river of living water whose source is in the Son: "He that believeth in me, as the scripture saith, *Out of his belly shall flow rivers of living water*" (7:38).

Similarly, in most cases, the Spirit is presented as proceeding both from the Father and the Son. This appears in a series of texts that are seldom brought together, describing the mysterious counsels of the Three Persons during the ten days that separate the Ascension of Christ from the outpouring of the Spirit—texts that are full of a silence like that which preceded the creation of the world. But these passages enable us to glimpse something of that "hidden mystery accomplished in the silence of God." The only begotten Son, raised to the right hand of the Father in His glorified humanity, prays to the Father that "he shall give you another Paraclete, that he may abide with you for ever" (*John*, 14:16). The equivalence of these two Comforters already signifies that they belong to the same nature. Elsewhere, we have already seen that the Spirit can only be given by the Father, from whom it proceeds, but not without the mediation of the Son.

Thus the Spirit is sent by the Father, but in the Name of the Son—and this is a new term, referring to its twofold procession: "The Father will send the Paraclete in my name" (*John*, 14:26). We may note here that the Father is always present as the origin, but the Son is always associated with Him, in a procession resembling the mission of the Spirit, and this makes it clear that the Spirit proceeds from both these Persons, but according to the proper nature of each of them. Another text, not this time from *St. John,* describes the Pentecost itself as the sending of the Spirit by the Son, in dependence on the Father: "Being exalted therefore by the right hand of God, and having received of the Father the promise of the Holy Ghost, he hath poured forth this which you see and hear" (*Acts*, 2:33).

But the words of Christ in *St. John's Gospel* already announced this outpouring of the Spirit in its twofold relationship with the Father and the Son: "When the Paraclete cometh, whom I will send you from the Father, the Spirit of truth, who proceedeth from the Father, he shall give testimony

of me" (*John*, 15:26). We return again and
again to this twofold dependence and this order in
dependence, whose primary origin is always hidden
in the Father, though it is nevertheless the Son
who is immediately responsible for sending the
Spirit. This order of mission is a reflection of that
of possession. So it is with justice that, in the
vision which we have been quoting, and which dominates the Johannine writings, the Spirit is presented
in the eternal outpouring of its existence and not
merely in its Pentecostal descent, which is the created reflection of the "a river of water of life,
clear as crystal, proceeding from the throne of
God and of the Lamb" (*Apoc.*, 22:1).

BIBLIOGRAPHY

Jules Lebreton, *Le Dieu Vivant*, 1919.
Jacques Dupont, *Essai sur la christologie de Saint Jean*, 1951.
M.-E. Boismard, *Le Prologue de Saint Jean*, 1953.

5

THE GOD OF
the Church

In the previous chapter we considered the new fact that is the essence of the New Testament, namely the revelation of the Trinity of Persons through the Incarnation of the Word and the outpouring of the Spirit. But we considered this new reality only in its existential aspect, as a decisive event in the history of salvation. The question now arises as to how we can have access to it—*i.e.* in what way we can attain knowledge of the Threefold God Who is revealed in the events of the New Testament. As the meaning of these events cannot be immediately grasped, the certainty that we have of them and their significance can only rest on testimony, as we established above. The authority of this testimony, to provide a basis for absolute certainty, should be a divine authority.

This brings us to a new class of questions, no longer connected with the examining of wise pagans or philosophers, but with the problems that divide Christians. The question is, in fact, whether the authority on which we base our certainty with regard to the Trinity of Persons in God is Scripture alone, or whether it is the evidence of a community assisted by the Spirit of God, and expressed both through Scripture and through living Tradition. It is clear that Scripture provides the fundamental guidance with regard to the revelation of the divine Persons in the work of salvation. But is Scripture, for all that, the sole source of this knowledge? Two problems arise here which we must deal with in succession. The first is that of the evidence of the Church and of living Tradition, insofar as it is the direct and infallible source of the knowledge of the Threefold God; the second is that of the part which the human mind plays in explaining the data of Scripture and Tradition—*i.e.* the function of theology.

The New Testament gives us the Revelation of the Trinity. This Revelation, constituted both by the teaching and the Person of Christ, was entrusted by Him to the Apostles. The writings of the New Testament transmit to us the teaching of the Apostles. But, once handed down to the Apostles, the authorized guardianship and promulgation of that teaching continues to belong to their successors. Thus it is through the Church, the infallible organ of Tradition, that the revelation of Christ is transmitted to us. However, this is challenged by Protestantism, which recognizes only the authority of Apostolic times, alike as the source of truth through Scripture and as the sole source of salvation through Redemption. There is no room for sacraments, nor for tradition. The Time of the Church has no salvational content. It is the function of the Church that we must now define more clearly.

Let us take, for example, the position of Cullmann, who stands midway between the radical Protestant position which we have described, and the Catholic position.[1] Against the Protestants, Cullmann admits that "through the Church, the history of salvation continues on earth . . . The sacraments extend the miracles accomplished by Jesus Christ in the time of the Incarnation (pp. 47-48). The work of the Incarnate Christ is pursued in His Church . . . There is not a void between the Ascension of Christ and His return . . . The revelation of the Word of God is continued in the Church" (pp. 53-54). I have quoted passages that show how nearly, as he himself recognizes, Cullmann's position approaches the Catholic perspective. All these passages would be accepted by Catholics, except the last, which would seem even to them to go too far.

But at the same time Cullmann wishes to preserve the absolutely privileged character of Apostolic times. This argument appeared already at the center of his *Christ et le Temps*. Cullmann reiterates it here: "If we consider the Christian faith from the angle of time, we shall say that the scandal of the Christian faith is to believe that those few years which, for profane history, were no more nor less than other periods, are the norm and center of the totality of all." But Cullmann criticizes Catholics for reducing this contrast. Consequently "the institution of the Apostolate, unique in the history of salvation, appears to be devalued by the infallible magisterium of the Church" (p. 55).

Let us first recognize the positive contribution of Cullmann's thought. The existence of a Time of the Church, during which the history of salvation is continued, is taken for granted.[2] It is clear that this brings Cullmann close to Catholicism. I should go further. In considering the realities of the Church as events in the history of salvation, Cullmann helps us to establish a theology of the history of the Church which we have often found wanting although St. Augustine has already explained that the catechesis, conceived as the history of salvation, comprehends the *praesentia tempora*.[3] Our theology of the Church is too often either purely speculative or merely anecdotal. Cullmann helps us to recover the idea of the Church as a historical epoch.

But once the existence of a Time of the Church is established, the question is to decide the extent of this Time. Cullmann criticizes Catholics for exaggerating it at the expense of the unique character of Apostolic times. We shall reply that Catholic theology recognizes a privileged character in Apostolic times. Indeed, with them the time of revelation, strictly speaking, is closed. There is, then, an essential difference between Apostolic and ecclesiastical times; and this difference has a bearing on the content of revelation. From this point of view, the Catholic Church resolutely sets aside the idea of new revelations. It is inaccurate to say, as Cullmann does, that "in the justification of the dogma

of the Assumption the Church considers that collective inspiration no longer needs to be controlled
by Apostolic testimony" (p. 55).

Where, then, does the difference lie? It appears
in this, that for Cullmann the distinction between
Apostolic and ecclesiastical times does not reside primarily in content. He seems even to admit that "the
revelation of the Word of God continues in the
Church" (p. 54). But the distinction is in the authority. For Cullmann, the doctrine of the Apostles
has a divine authority which is imposed absolutely
on faith; in the Church, the Holy Spirit is always
at work; the Church has an authority, but that
authority cannot be normative. It must always be
submitted to the one and only norm, which is Apostolic doctrine. The Church demands our respect.
It would be unwise to misunderstand her, but
she does not require the support of our faith. "To
assert the unique character of the revelation granted
to the Apostles, is not to deny the value of all
post-Apostolic tradition, but it is clearly to bring
tradition down to the level of a human datum,
even though the Holy Spirit can be revealed also
through it" (p. 51).

Accordingly the Church will have the right and
the duty to proclaim that which, in the light of the
Apostolic norm, appears to her to be revelation.
Thus the Apostolic tradition is developed. This
tradition will have a great value for the Church,
and Protestantism is wrong to underestimate it in
principle: "But whatever be the respect which the
Church owes to tradition, and the importance of

tradition in the elaboration and comprehension of Christian doctrine, it can never have the same value as the Apostolic norm, still less can it become that norm" (p. 54). Up to this point, it is clear that Cullman follows Catholic theology. He acknowledges a development of doctrine, inspired by the Holy Spirit. But this development preserves the character of a human tradition, which can always be brought into question.

We are now at the center of the controversy, and a host of questions crop up. The first is that of the respective value of the authority of Scripture and of the Church. But here there is an ambiguity in Cullmann's thinking, which reappears in his book on St. Peter. On the one hand, Cullmann presupposes in the beginning a primacy of the Church over Scripture. Christ wrote nothing, yet it would have been easy for Him to do so. Mani scored an easy victory on this point by declaring that he, at least, had put all his teaching in written form. But the objection is too easy to be worth making. If Christ wrote nothing, this is doubtless because He did not wish to write anything. He entrusted His message not to dead books, but to living men, to a Church, whose duty was to transmit it.

Cullmann admits this. But we see that after Apostolic times the perspective is reversed. This time it is no longer a living community that dispenses authority, but once again written books. Cullmann will reply that these books preserve a privileged stage in the tradition. But we must make a distinction. We agree that the fixing of the Canon marks the end of revelation properly so called. But we question whether this transfers the seat of authority and makes it pass from the living Church to the written letter. The only change is that the post-Apostolic Church transmits a received deposit, but transmits it with a sovereign authority. It is she who remains the repository of infallible authority. The Gospel remains the living tradition of the message.

However, Cullmann seems to have sensed the difficulty. The problem is not that of the oneness of the Apostolate; we are all agreed on that. But the problem is rather the embodiment of the Apostolate: "How are we to embody for ourselves this testimony which God has granted, for the salvation of the world, to the Apostles, in the period that we call the center of time?" (p. 51). To this Cullmann replies that "the Apostle should himself continue to fulfil his function in the Church today" (p. 53). And how is he to do so? By his writings. But this seems to me altogether ambiguous. Cullmann rejects the embodiment of the Apostolic tradition in the Church, because he considers that it runs the risk of adulteration. But embodiment in Scripture presents a parallel difficulty, that of error in interpretation. In every way, there is a human intermediary, whether he be a teacher or a reader.

This criterion, therefore, does not seem to me to have any theological value for distinguishing the instrument in which the Apostolic message is embodied. It arises from something else, from that taste for direct contact with Scripture which is characteristic of Protestantism, and whose value is in any case unquestionable. Cullmann remarks that this taste is in fact developing in Catholicism, and he is right to be pleased about this. He expresses his pleasure very rightly when he says: "Don't we always feel a renewed sense of liberation when, after ploughing through piles of commentaries, we turn back to the Word of the Bible itself?" (p. 66). I quite agree that I have just the same feeling; but is this really the point at issue?

If by tradition we mean the commentaries through which succeeding generations have tried to interpret Scripture, it is certainly clear that this tradition, being nothing but an accumulation of human inquiries, however directed by the Spirit, can only provide a screen, which must be continually cleared away in order that we may renew our contact with the text itself. But this seems to be just as much Cullmann's position. His outlook is one of exegesis. His reliance on Scripture is a return to the source, the need to get into touch again with the original document beyond all the glosses. Once again, this is quite legitimate. But then we have the impression that we are talking about different things when we speak of tradition.

Moreover, it seems to us that Cullmann himself is using the word "tradition" in two different senses when he speaks of Apostolic tradition and ecclesiastical tradition. In the first phrase, the word tradition has theological value; it means the help given by God to the Christian community, which preserves it from error. This is a biblical datum, as we shall show. In the second case, tradition—it would be better to say, traditions—are composed of the human glosses that are made on Scripture. Cullmann himself likens these traditions to those of the rabbis or to the secret traditions of the Gnostics (pp. 64-65). But it is clear that in the first case tradition dominates Scripture, which is only its written record, while in the second case it is, on all the evidence, secondary in relation to Scripture.

But the question arises whether this change of meaning, when we pass from Apostolic to ecclesiastical tradition, is legitimate. What is certain is that this is precisely what Catholicism does not accept; and it does not accept it because it sees no reason to confine the theological meaning of "tradition" to the time of the Apostles. In fact, Tradition in the theological sense—as we have seen, the fact that Christ entrusted His message not to written books but to living men—seems to Catholics an absolutely general characteristic of God's plan, which is already to be found in the Old Testament, and is an aspect of the theology of the Covenant.

But to this Cullmann might reply that this privilege in the Old Covenant is restricted to what it was at the time of revelation. Also it is found again in the New Covenant during the time of the Apostles, which is a time of Revelation. It ceased as soon as this period came to an end. It is the Church herself that infallibly renounced infallibility in fixing the Canon: "We may risk the paradoxical statement that the magisterium of the Church approaches real infallibility to the extent that, in submitting the Canon, she abandoned all *claim* to infallibility" (p. 63). But we can see where the ambiguity lies. The Church, by fixing the Canon, brought Revelation to an end, but not infallibility. We come to the fundamental point. The difference between Apostolic and ecclesiastical times is that between revelation and tradition, not between infallibility and fallibility. The Church is as infallible in transmitting the deposit as the Apostles were in revealing it.

Thus infallibility does not mean revelation, but strictly divine action. The question is solely that of knowing whether God works in the New people of God as He worked in the Old. The sign of the presence of God in the Old Israel was its infallibility in the transmission of the Word of God. But, for Cullmann, there is no infallibility in the New Israel. There is the help of the Spirit, but nowhere does it guarantee freedom from error. The authority of the people of the Old Covenant was a divine authority, the authority of the Church is a human authority. Under these conditions Cullmann cannot maintain that the history of salvation continues effectively in the Church. He is brought back willynilly to the traditonal Protestant position.

Yet his statements to the contrary are too explicit for us to leave the matter at that. Besides, there is a similar case where Cullmann, this time, does not hesitate to describe the Time of the Church as a sequel to that of the Incarnation; it is the case of the sacraments. Here Cullmann's position is quite straightforward: "We hold that the sacraments, baptism and the eucharist, occupy in the Church the place that the miracles of Jesus Christ occupy in the time of the Incarnation" (p. 48). But the miracles of Jesus Christ are divine acts. The sacraments are equally so. They infallibly bring into action the participation of the dead and resurrected Christ.[4]

But this continuity with the time of the Incarnation, which Cullmann admits in the case of the sacraments, and which is logical from his standpoint, he denies in the case of the Word. The characteristic of divine action which he recognizes in the sacraments, he denies to the teachings. We must ask why this is so. Cullmann will reply that it is because we seem to him to minimize in this way the privileged character of the time of the Incarnation and the oneness of the Apostolate. But this would apply quite as much to the sacraments; and this is precisely the criticism that the Protestants make. For a consistent Protestantism, the sacraments are a representation, not an embodiment, of redemptive action in Jesus Christ.

But Cullmann goes beyond this position, as far as the sacraments are concerned. He sees clearly that they are not merely juxtaposed to the unique redemptive action, but embody it, render it effectively present in all times. Why, then, does he not admit this with regard to the teachings of the Church? Here he speaks of juxtaposition. I think this is connected with his idea of Tradition, which for him is something that is added to revelation in the form of a commentary, a gloss, an interpretation. But this is secondary. These are human traditions which have in fact only a human value. But Tradition in the theological sense is another matter; it is the transmission of revelation. Just as the sacraments are the embodiment of the unique act of salvation, so Tradition is the embodiment of the unique act of revelation.

We see here that the Catholic conception of Tradition by no means suppresses the oneness of the Apostolate, to which Cullmann is rightly attached. Here again it is as with the sacraments. It is clear that there is no other act of salvation besides that of the death and resurrection of Jesus. The sacraments cannot, then, be another act of salvation. They are only that unique act rendered present, but in an effective manner—which effectiveness is divine. It is the same with Revelation. There is only one Revelation, the one made to the Apostles. It is perfectly clear, then, that the time of the Revelation is a uniquely privileged historical time. But this Revelation is rendered infallibly present through the action of God in the Time of the Church by the magisterium.

It remains true that there is a difference between the embodiment of the redemption in the sacraments and that of revelation in the magisterium. If they both presuppose a Church, it remains true that the infallibility of the magisterium has a stricter relationship with the unity of the Church. For her to act, there must be a visible connection to which God has attached His authority. To recognize the existence of a tradition in the Catholic sense is to recognize the infallibility of the successor of Peter. Cullmann has no doubt foreseen this conclusion. In any case it enables us to understand why his book on St. Peter and the article we have been discussing have such a close connection.

But whatever these motives may be, it remains true that we must submit to facts. Yet is there not a case in which there is an embodiment of revelation that provides a normative value? Cullmann recognizes that there is such a case, that of the rule of faith. He recognizes, too, that this has a normative value. But is not this at once to admit a norm other than Scripture? No, replies Cullmann, for the rule of faith is itself part of Apostolic times. "We do not find on one side the Apostles' Creed, and on the other their writings. But both form a single whole, as Apostolic tradition confronting post-Apostolic. The Apostles' Creed was, as it were, a summary of the books of the New Testament. In order to become a norm for interpretation, this Creed must itself be Apostolic" (pp. 63-64).

The problem seems far less simple than this. For here Cullmann's reasoning assumes that the rule of faith, called the Apostles' Creed, is of Apostolic origin. But nothing is less certain. The recent work of J. N. Kelly[5] has shown that the first formulations were more varied in form than Cullmann imagined.[6] The Apostles' Creed seems to be the Roman baptismal creed of the second century. But it is one such symbol among several. It already represents, no doubt, a dogmatic development in relation to the New Testament. Moreover, it includes later additions, the communion of saints, the descent into hell.

This is an important question. For here is a text whose normative character Cullmann recognizes; yet it is difficult to maintain its Apostolic character. Are we not face to face here with that embodiment of written revelation which is not juxtaposed to it, but appears as its vital expression? Yet it is precisely its development that characterizes the formulation of faith. The Creed is the expression of the official interpretation by the Church of the written revelation. Unlike the Scriptures of the New Testament, its authority does not derive from the Apostles, as Cullmann claims, but from the Church. It represents the official and infallible expression of her faith.

The consideration of the formulation of faith, therefore, seems to me of capital importance to the present discussion. The Apostles' Creed, however, does not seem to be separable from later symbols. There are no natural differences between them. Their sum-total, which it would be necessary to complete with dogmatic definitions, constitutes strictly and exclusively the authentic Tradition—*i.e.* the authorized interpretation of Scripture. The question arises as to what authority is attributed to them. If Cullmann admits the normative value of the Apostles' Creed, even in the case where its Apostolic character is excluded, he recognizes implicitly the normative value of the substance of Tradition. Such is the conception of Apostolic Tradition which seems to us to correspond to the teaching of the New Testament. This suffices for our proof; but we can find confirmation of it in the fact that this conception is that which we encounter in the second century in St. Irenaeus, whose connections, moreover, with the Apostolic milieu are well established. The vocabulary of the Tradition in his work has been exhaustively studied by Dom Reynders[7] and Père Holstein.[8] The results to which their researches lead are very remarkable. The verb *paradidonai*, which expresses the Tradition as an act of transmission is, says Dom Reynders, "exclusively confined" to the Apostles (*loc. cit.*, p. 188). Père Holstein varies this statement slightly, but it remains substantially true. Let us quote one example among many: "The Apostles transmitted to all, that which they themselves had learnt from Our Lord" (*Adv. haer.*, III, 14, 2). It is, then, incontestable that the Apostles were considered as the source of Tradition in an altogether privileged manner.

But if we now take the noun *paradosis*, which means tradition as a thing transmitted, we may be certain that the Apostles are never its subject-matter, but always the Church. Thus "the Church throughout the world has received this tradition from the Apostles" (II, 9, 1). We shall find the complete extract in Dom Reynders' article (pp. 180, 181). It is especially noteworthy that in the majority of the passages it is a question of the Apostles *and* the Church, the former considered as communicating the Tradition and the latter as receiving it.

This close connection makes it clear that it is the same tradition that is referred to under two aspects, its origin and its subject-matter. Père Holstein is right to declare, after having compared the texts: "This extract well demonstrates the Apostolic and Church character of the Irenaean tradition: more precisely, for it is not a question of a two-fold tradition, but of the Apostolic character of Church Tradition" (*loc. cit.*, p. 235). Thus, for Irenaeus, it is clear that the distinction between an Apostolic and an ecclesiastical tradition is entirely absent from his work.

As for the place of Tradition and the Apostolic Succession, it is fairly well known that this is a favorite theme of Irenaeus. The Kerygma, *i.e.* the proclamation which the Apostles officially made of the Revelation, is immediately fixed by them in the Scriptures (*Adv. haer.*, III, 1, 1) and transmitted in the person of their successors: "We appeal on this matter to the tradition which comes from the Apostles and is preserved in their Churches through the succession of the presbyters" (III, 2, 2). This preservation of the Kerygma in the Tradition has an authority equal to that of the Scriptures, to the point where it alone could be sufficient: "If the Apostles themselves had not left any Scriptures, would we not be obliged to follow the rule of the Tradition which they left to those to whom they entrusted the Churches?" (III, 4, 1). We see that this is opposed to Cullmann's idea, which regards the writings of the New Testament as the fixing of the Tradition of Apostolic times. For Irenaeus, Scripture and Tradition are both directly connected with the Apostles and enjoy equal authority.

But the object of this Tradition is primarily the proclamation of the Three Persons. Irenaeus is absolutely explicit on this point. He concludes his summary of the Tradition, insofar as it is distinguished from Scripture, with a summary of its content: "They carefully guard the ancient Tradition, believing in only one God, Creator of heaven and earth and all that therein is, through Jesus Christ, the Son of God, who, in the greatness of His love, consented to be born of the Virgin, who suffered under Pontius Pilate, was raised up, was received in glory, will come in glory, Judge of those who are judged, Savior of those who are saved. Those who, without Scripture, have believed this faith, God will not reject." (*Adv. haer.*, III, 4, 2).

This summary is familiar to us; it is equivalent to our Apostles' Creed, or to our Nicene Creed. We know that this summary passed through many forms before being fixed. But the essential features are always the same. It represents the program of the catachesis. In Irenaeus it has a characteristic name, "the canon of truth": "He that rightly holds within him this canon of truth which he received at baptism, shall know the names (*i.e.* the Three Persons) that come from the Scriptures" (*Adv. haer.*, I, 9, 4). Faith in the Trinity is, then, the deposit left by Christ Himself to His Church to be preserved intact and maintained against all distortions. It is this that is transmitted officially at baptism through a living and authorized Tradition throughout all generations.

The Church does nothing but transmit this faith in the Trinity. The Tradition, according to a useful phrase of Moeller, is a living Tradition. This means that the Church has infallible power to define, in the face of any errors of interpretation that may appear, the authentic content of Revelation. Such, as regards the Trinity, were the definitions of the Council of Nicaea and Constantinople, which maintained the perfect equality of the Three Persons in the face of the Arian heresy. This means equally that the Church has the power to clarify this or that aspect of Revelation. She uses for this purpose the work of theologians.

Thus Scripture and Tradition are the sources that give us access to Revelation. But this datum once revealed, man's intellect sets to work according to the manner proper to it, which is rational and discursive. "It is not a case of a rational activity setting to work on the datum of faith, but of the light of faith informing and using reason." [9] This search is the purpose of theology, which is, according to St. Anselm's phrase, *"fides quaerens intellectum,"* the faith that seeks to understand its object. This leads us to a new class of questions that are concerned with the reflections by which the human intellect, illuminated by revelation, vivified by grace, attempts to fathom the datum of revelation.

The usefulness of theology has often been challenged in the course of the history of Christen-

dom. Why, it will be said first of all, should we
not keep scrupulously close to Revelation, as it is
set forth by the Bible and Tradition? Do we not
run the risk of substituting human speculations for
the word of God by seeking to reason about it?
Besides, it will be added, the form in which the
Bible and the Tradition set forth Revelation, as the
proclamation of salvation and its means, is surely
the form in which the truths of the faith ought to
be presented. It constitutes "kerygmatic" theology,
which is the only one of any value. Moreover, by
wishing to be too systematic about revealed truths,
do we not run the risk of impoverishing them, of
reducing to definitions and deductions the living
fullness of the Word of God? Does not the intel-
lectualism of theology run the risk of misleading
men who are looking for a God who is felt by
the heart, for religious experience? Is there not
even a danger of emptying the mystery itself, and
substituting for it a rational system?

These criticisms are not without value, and the
history of theology shows that it has to some extent
deserved them. It is true, in fact, that theology can
add nothing to the deposit of Tradition and Scripture, since Revelation came to an end in Apostolic
times. It must be said, too, that the normal form
of the presentation of the Christian message is the
preaching of the Word, the Kerygma, and that it
is a mistake to substitute theological discussions for
this. It must be recognized that the fullness of
Revelation, as it is contained in Scripture and Tradition, overflows all theology, and that this is an

inventory which is always incomplete. It is equally
true that theology is inadequate if it does not end
in mysticism, *i.e.* in a living encounter with the
living God. Finally it is true that theologies have
often sinned through rationalism. The most famous
example is one of the oldest and greatest of theologians, Origen, about whom there is still a controversy as to whether his system is philosophical
or theological, whether its first principles are taken
from revelation or from reason.[10]

There may be abuses in theology. It is important
to place it correctly among those ways of understanding God which we are studying in this book,
in order to show at the same time its value and
its limitations. First, as to its value. We have said
that Revelation, as it is presented to us by Scripture and Tradition, refers essentially to facts. In
it we see God dealing with concrete situations,
making a covenant, judging, freeing. In the New
Testament we see Christ acting as God, the Spirit
performing miracles. But these facts may at first
be misunderstood. The history of Christendom provides evidence of this. It is only necessary to watch
the gropings of the first Christians when they are
speaking of the Trinity, their hesitations as to the
right way of expressing the relationship of the
Word to the Father. Four centuries must elapse
before Nicaea gives an exact formulation of the
doctrine of the Trinity.

So it is especially true that those who wish to
keep to the strict letter of the Bible and suppress
the refinements of theology, run the risk of them-

selves falling into confusion and uncertainty. The experience of such reliance on the Bible alone makes this clear. Certainly there has been in Lutheranism a legitimate thirst for direct contact with the Word of God beyond the Colossus of mediaeval theology and the sterile arguments of decadent scholasticism. But in eliminating theology, they eliminated also at the same time the progress of dogmatic tradition. By making Scripture alone the source of truth, they were exposed to all the false currents that followed, for everyone interpreted Scripture in his own way. Certainly, as we have said, it was to the Church that Christ entrusted His message. This is what makes possible dogmatic definitions. But these definitions presuppose all the labors of theology.

It is quite true that contact with the Bible and Tradition is always necessary. Nothing is so dangerous as to substitute for this contact any kind of theological systematization. The Bible and Tradition are the regulative bases to which the theologian must always refer, on pain of making arbitrary constructions. When it throws out ballast, theology loses contact with the very reality that is its object, and is dissipated in clouds of speculation. But this does not mean that theology is not also necessary. For it is the labor of the intellect which, by bringing the revealed data together, by noting their connections, prevents revelation from remaining in a crude and muddled state, clarifies the data and thus permits a better understanding of them. Moreover, the Bible and Tradition do not exist in the pure state. Since comment on them began, they

have been interpreted, and thus the study of theology has developed. To despise theology is only to
introduce poor theology.

But, it will be said, the problem is not the
theoretical one of theology as such. It is a problem
of fact. Is it not true that Revelation is deformed
after it has been interpreted by theologians? They
have indeed, in their attempts to express Revelation,
borrowed philosophical classifications that belonged
to Plato and Aristotle. By interpreting the Word
of God through these classifications, have they not
established a kind of gnosis? Is not the theology
of Origen a type of Christian Platonism, rather
than a true theology? Has not the use of Aristotelian categories by St. Thomas twisted Revelation,
by substituting the categories of matter and form,
act and power, for the biblical categories of *b'rith*
and *emet, tsedeq* and *hesed?* Must we not free ourselves from these categories and return to those of
the Bible?

We have shown throughout the previous chapter
how well-founded this remark is. Certainly when
using the word *logos* to translate the biblical *dabar*,
St. John exposed Christian theology to great difficulties. For *logos* connoted in Greek philosophy a
number of rationalist and pantheist aspects which
it was at first difficult to cast aside; hence the
numerous errors of the pioneer theologians in this
field. Similar comments might be made on the
translation of *ruah* by *pneuma,* or *tsedeq* by *iustitia.*
However, this no longer bears on the problem of
theology, but that of the passing of revelation from

one linguistic scale to another. Yet this is an extremely delicate and dangerous undertaking. Even today, as we have seen, it occasionally produces misunderstandings!

But first of all, if this is a delicate task, it is not, for all that, one which involves twisting or deforming. In fact, by using philosophical terms to formulate the realities of revelation, theology endows them with fresh content. Translation from Hebrew into Greek was necessary, since the Gospel was to be preached to all peoples. This translation involved the risk of misunderstanding. That is why the development of new theological categories was necessary; and in fact this is just what was produced. After some centuries theology found itself confronting new ideas—person, substance, nature— borrowed materially from Greek, but having taken on a meaning of their own which enabled the theologians to formulate the revelation in Greek terms.

This brings us to the fact that there is a confusion among those who wish to "stick to the Bible"; for biblical categories have two possible meanings.[11] On the one hand, there are the intelligible terms themselves, in which Revelation is expressed; and on the other hand there is the Semitic form which they took in the Bible. But it must be said that the second aspect is secondary. Hebrew was not part of Revelation. Revelation transcends every possible culture, and should be expressed in every language in the world. This is not deformity, but enrichment. For to express the unique truth of

Revelation in terms of different cultures is to throw different aspects into relief. We conclude from this, on a theological basis, that far from contesting the legitimacy of expressing Revelation in terms of Greek philosophy as theologians have done, it must be said that what is to be hoped today is precisely that this task may be undertaken for India and China.[12]

Moreover, theology enables us to disentangle the true meaning of Revelation from erroneous interpretations which have been made of it. History arises to a great extent from the reality of heresy. The first theologians, Irenaeus or Tertullian, wrote to refute the errors of the Gnostics and to show that they interpreted Scripture falsely. The great theologians of the Trinity in the fourth century, Athanasius, Gregory of Nazianzen, Gregory of Nyssa, refuted the errors of Arius and Eunomius with regard to the Trinity. The work of St. Augustine is largely a refutation of Pelagianism. The theologians of the sixteenth century developed a theology of grace and freedom in face of Protestant errors. Thus theology prepares the way for the magisterium of the Church, which alone has ultimate authority to define the Faith by virtue of the assistance of the Holy Spirit.

But this negative aspect is not the essential one. The purpose of the great theologians is to disentangle what is implied in the datum of Revelation. The latter, as we have said, appears as a testimony borne to divine acts. Theology will have as its object to show what these events reveal to us about

God. For instance, the Bible shows us God punishing adulterous Israel and displaying His jealousy. This is a concrete situation charged with many meanings; theology will demonstrate that it is a sign of monotheism, of the fact that divinity belongs exclusively to the unique and transcendent God. Similarly the Bible shows us Christ declaring that He is greater than the Sabbath, because God alone can change the Sabbath, which was established by God. Theology will show that this implies His divinity.

Theology must then define the meaning of these characteristics of the living God which it disentangles, for they are often ambiguous. Thus it is not enough to show that Christ is God, and then that there is in God someone other than the Father. It is necessary to show in what this distinction consists. For it can be understood in an excessive manner, in the sense of a duality of gods, which would reintegrate polytheism. This is what an ignorance of theology often causes non-Christians to say. But we may also sin by default through only seeing in the Word of God a power of God or a mode of His being. This is why theology will be led to maintain precisely that the Word of God is a Person, *i.e.* possesses a substance distinct from that of the Father, but yet that there is only one divine nature, possessed indissociably by the Father and the Son.

It is clear that, in its attempt to understand the mystery of God, theology remains the work of human intellect. If intellect really knows God in the revelation which He makes of Himself, intellect becomes aware of its limitations. This is why theology is not rationalist. It does not explain the mystery of God in the sense that it renders it wholly intelligible. It knows the mystery as a mystery; but it proclaims it in an exact manner. Thus theology does not explain how it is possible for there to be Three Persons in God. This remains an unfathomable mystery, which even the vision of the angels cannot penetrate. But it declares that there are Three Persons in God, and thus theology passes beyond what can be known by reason.

Finally, these data which theology clarifies, beginning with Scripture and Tradition, are shown in their order and their connections. Christian knowledge is made up of correspondences between the various fields of faith. It is not an explanation and a justification of Revelation through anything other than Revelation. The Word of God is its unique and exclusive point of departure. But it is an inventory of the riches of the Word of God, disentangling them to discover the unity of the divine plan; and it is this very unity that is itself its own justification. For there is in the convergence of all the data and in their connection an authentic testimony which comes to light. It is the totality of Revelation that proves every detail of Revelation; and it is the task of theology to demonstrate this totality.

Thus we see the connection between theology and the datum of revelation. Theology is simply the knowledge of Scripture and Tradition. It should not be separated from them. It is to the Word of God that the theologian must always return. But at the same time the Word of God is clarified by theology; its obscurities are cleared away, its difficulties are resolved, its unity is discovered amid diversity. There has no doubt been in the last few centuries too great a dissociation between a too purely scientific exegesis and a too exclusively rational theology. The reunion of exegesis with theology is necessary to the enrichment of both.

We have not, with this, exhausted the content of theology. It is, as we have said, the attempt of the intellect to understand the datum of revelation. But this attempt, if it is the task of reason, is not the task of a purely natural reason, but of a reason vivified by grace. Theology is the work of faith. Faith, in fact, is not only the act by which the mind cleaves to the testimony of the Word in its mysterious content. It is also a divine, supernatural virtue, which raises the mind above itself and joins it to the nature of the mystery.[13] It is a new intellect, created by the Spirit, Who alone fathoms the depths of God and enables the intellect to grasp these realities in an obscure but real manner.

This new intellect is at first rudimentary, but, as it comes into play, it gradually grows more luminous; it shares in the knowledge which God has of Himself. The intellect is already a rough sketch of the vision; only the veils of the flesh still blur the outlines. Developing through the gifts of the Holy Spirit, through the gift of science and the gift of understanding, the new intellect makes the mind familiar with divine realities, and enables it to

grasp them in all their fullness and to assess the
evidence which they present. If it is false to reduce
theology to the contemplation of faith, and to
eliminate its strictly rational aspect, it is equally
false to try to eliminate this new element and reduce it to a purely rational dialectic. Many fruitless
controversies have sprung from the wish to deny
one or other of these elements.

The function of what we may call "divining"
faith in theology is especially marked in the Fathers
of the Church. In the Greek Fathers, from Clement of Alexandria, we encounter the idea that faith
develops through gnosis; but they are simply re-
peating here a Pauline term. This gnosis has nothing esoteric about it. It has no other object than
faith. But it represents faith which has become
luminous and is engaged in contemplating its object. For Origen, theology appears as intellect in its
spiritual meaning as the Word of God, *i.e.* the hidden reality present beneath the apparent letter. This
idea was not without its dangers, in that it risked
misunderstanding the primacy of the literal meaning. But it justly expresses the fact that Scripture
alone shows in their emergence in the history of
salvation the hidden realities of the eternal God
and of the spiritual creation, which are for Origen
the final object of theology. For Origen's disciple
Evagrus, *theologia* is the summit of the contemplative ascent, the very vision of the Trinity.

Among the Fathers, this conception of theology is
often accompanied by a depreciation of dialectic.[14]
They criticize the Arians, the technologists, the use

of Aristotelian categories. St. Thomas Aquinas re-
acted against the dangers that might be incurred
by a too purely contemplative theology. He restored
reasoning to its place in theology, and did not
hesitate, despite the dismay which this at first
aroused in conservative theological circles, to use
Aristotelian categories. As it turned out, this revo-
lution was a liberation. For, as we have said, reason plays an essential part in the inward life of
theology. But St. Thomas was also a man of
prayer; therefore his theology, scientific and rational as it is, remains at the same time divining
and contemplative.

This was not always true of decadent scholasticism. The abuse of dialectic, the framing of useless
questions, the virtuosity of reason, often give the
impression that it has lost sight of the seriousness
of its purpose. Père de Balthasar was right to
maintain that, in patristic times, theological speculation and the contemplative life went hand in
hand, that the doctors of the Church were saints,
while, in modern times, theologians are not always
saints, and saints are not in every case theologians.[15]
A certain sterility in modern theology is chiefly due
to the fact that the supernatural sap, the dynamism
of faith toward the vision of the Trinity, no
longer animates it. The true science of God is that
which leads us to love God. It is impossible to read
St. Augustine without being struck by the impulse
that draws him towards the Trinity. The same cannot always be said of our contemporary guide-
books.

For, after all, if we have said that philosophy, when it meets the mystery of God, must be converted and become open to worship, it is only just that we should demand as much of the theologian. But the latter often settles down in the world of revelation as if it were his private residence. He gossips about it like any other subject. He treats it without that spirit of deep reverence which we should expect by right when it is a matter of the living God. But is it really of God that he is chattering? Are not these merely empty concepts that he accumulates, since all true knowledge is grasped from the authentic reality of things through the mediation of the concept? And how can one grasp the reality of God without the illumination of faith? Theology therefore appears to us in its rightful place among the ways of knowing God. It presupposes Scripture and Tradition—they are the starting-points of its undertaking. Theology is the attempt of intellect in various forms to comprehend and formulate the datum which Revelation presents in the crude state. It meets at the opposite pole the mystical knowledge of God, in that it is illuminated by divining faith, which glimpses, however obscurely, the very reality of the mystery.

The word "theology" means in current speech the sum-total of speculation on the datum of revelation, whether it be that of God or of grace, or of the Church, or of the sacraments. The Fathers, more strictly, distinguished Theology properly so called, which refers to the divine Persons and the Economy that stems from them, from the work of God in the creation and the redemption. It is in this sense that we use the word here, since God is the only subject of this book. Theology refers at once to God in His essence and in His Persons. We shall leave on one side the first aspect, because we have had occasion to examine it several times, particularly in relation to the Revelation of God in the Covenant. We shall content ourselves with saying that it must be distinguished from theodicy, or the philosophical knowledge of God. We are concerned, rather, with the divine nature, as Revelation has enabled us to know it. But our object will be solely that of the theology of the Trinity.

It is clear that we cannot, in the course of a few pages, define what constitutes the very heart of theology. We should only wish to show, as our object is here, the nature of theological knowledge and the problems which it encounters. Thus we are simply continuing what we began in the previous chapter. We had indicated that Revelation shows us the Three Persons revealing themselves as divine and as personal through missions, the Father sending the Son and the Spirit, and the Son and the Spirit revealing themselves in the works which they accomplish. Theology extends Revelation by disentangling from this essential manifestation what are the eternal relationships between the Three Persons.

We must recognize the formidable nature of this undertaking, in order to understand with what difficulties it is beset. The human mind is in fact confronted here with a totally alien reality, to which it has no point of reference in its experience, and which seems even to challenge all the principles that are at its disposal in this class of experience. The brightness of the Trinity is so blinding that human sight cannot focus on it. All that is available to the mind is the data of Scripture, which must be interpreted by those data themselves. So, tremblingly comparing text with text, the mind advances in this unknown and unknowable world, in which it has no bearings other than those that the Trinity Itself has permitted to be glimpsed of Its activity in the world. It is through stammerings, whose imperfection the mind perceives only too clearly, that it may arrive at sound formulations.

For we must begin with the fact that the very basis of the Christian Faith is that there is only one God. This statement pervades the Old Testament, and provides the unshakable basis of biblical faith. In the presence of the one only God, the New Testament reveals the existence of the Son who is God and the Spirit who is God. The starting-point of theology, in her effort to unite these two statements, will be to declare that it is true that there is only one God, in that there is a sense in which the one God alone possesses divinity in the original and primordial sense, and that this God is the Father. But the Son and the Spirit are really God, in that they really possess divinity, but in a secondary and derivative manner. We do not see how we could have begun to formulate things in any other way. This is certainly what the pioneer theologians did, when they dared to look the problem in the face.

Thus the Judaeo-Christian theologians, using the familiar categories of the Judaism of the period, defined the Son and the Spirit as angels, meaning by this spiritual persons of a pre-eminent nature, distinct from the Father, but inferior to Him.[16] The first Greek theologians express themselves in a more speculative manner. Justin sees in the Father the hidden and inaccessible God, in the Word the manifestation of God to humanity. Thus appears a feature which will long remain characteristic of the theology of the Word—its relation to creation. For Origen, although he was the first to attempt to express more rigorously the mode of generation of the Word, the latter remained separated from the Father by an abyss comparable with that which separated Him from creation. Moreover, the Father is pure unity, the Word is at once one and many, being thus intermediate between the Father, who alone is *ho theos,* and the creation of which He is the archetype.

Latin theology provides a similar formulation. For Tertullian, the Word has eternally existed, as immanent and impersonal thought, in God, in that God is mind and therefore thought. But the Word only took on personal subsistence when He was proffered as the instrument of creation. Thus He is eternal as thought, but not as a Person. Conversely, Origen, who admitted the eternity of the Word as a Person, but regarded His relationship with the world as one of essence, was consequently led to conclude that the world was eternal. We can understand the reason for these gropings. The existence of the Word, as we have said, appears in revelation on the occasion of His missions in Creation and in the Incarnation; hence the tendency to connect these missions with His Person, not to consider Him apart from them in His eternal relationship with the Father. Tertullian, moreover, imprisoned in representations which were still material, saw in the Son a portion of the Father's substance.

These difficulties, whose origins are to be found even in Scripture, were further increased by interference from the philosophical systems of the time, which attracted the theology of the Trinity to their orbit. Philosophers of the Platonic mean, such as Numenius and Albinus, conceived of the divinity as a hierarchy of hypostases. Plotinus gave the vision its most rigorous form by seeing Intellect as an emanation of the primordial One, and the soul in its turn as an emanation of Intellect. For this phase of expansion there was a corresponding phase of contraction, in which all returned to the primitive One. The greatest of the Arian theologians, Eunomus, applied a similar scheme to the Trinity. Identifying the aseity of the divine nature with the fact that the property of the Father is to be unbegotten, he confined aseity to the Father alone.

But already, in the form that Arius had given it, this picture of things had been felt to be unfaithful to the biblical datum, and as incompatible with the divinity of the Word. The latter did not simply possess a secondary, shared, divine nature. He had not received it by a free choice of the Father. But He possessed the same divine nature as the Father, in the same eternity. The Council of Nicaea sanctioned this statement, by defining the consubstantiality (*homo ousios*) of the Father and the Son, at the same time as their equal dignity and their equal eternity. But this statement in its turn was accepted with difficulty. To say that the Son had the same *ousia* as the Father, is surely to confound Him with the Father. The theological question was complicated by questions of vocabulary. The word *ousia* could just as well stand for the nature as the person. It was necessary to restrict it to mean the nature, and contrast it with another word, *hypostasis,* meaning the person.

Superficial minds may see here only a battle of words. But the Fathers of the Church were no fools. They knew how grave were the issues at stake in these discussions, and how fatal would be the consequences of error. If indeed the Son is not truly God, wrote St. Basil, human nature is not made divine by His Incarnation, and the divine life is not communicated at baptism. Thus it is the whole of Christian existence that is brought in question. For the doctrine of the Trinity is not an abstruse doctrine. The whole Christian life hangs upon it. It is at once the most mysterious and the most elementary of doctrines. It is in the Name of the Three Persons that an infant is baptized. He is plunged, as a tiny mite of flesh and blood, into the fullness of the life of the Trinity. All eternity will be only the unfolding of this initial grace.

The divinity of the Word is therefore the corner-stone on which all rests, apart from which every-thing breaks down. This is why we must at all costs succeed in defining it correctly.

Thus at Nicaea the fundamental statement was made of the total unity of the nature of the Father and the Son, of the distinction between their Persons. The Council of Constantinople, in 381, extended this definition to the Holy Spirit. But this left open the opposite difficulty of consubstantiality. If everything whatever is held in common between the Father, the Son, and the Spirit, what constitutes their formal differences and makes them specifically Persons? For They are not three identical Persons, if each has a unique nature. Such is the narrow ridge onto which the theologian had climbed. More-over, when he had established himself there, it appeared to him that, thanks to an astonishing para-dox, the only thing that was proper to each Person was His relationship with the others. The Father only exists in His relationship with the Son, and the Spirit in His relationship with the Father and the Son. At the same time there appeared in a clear light the reason for their eternal coexistence. If the Father only exists in His relationship with the Son, He necessarily coexists eternally with the Son. There is between the Three Persons a total interdepend-ence and a total mutuality.

This is the final word that can be spoken with certainty about that which remains ineffable. For, after having said that God is thus One and Three, we must repeat with Pseudo-Dionysus: "Thus the transcendent Deity celebrates together both as Unity and as Trinity. Indeed It is not knowable by us nor by any being, either as Unity or as Trinity. To celebrate in true reality that which in It is more One than the One Itself, that is to say that Principle which begets in Itself the divine realities, we attribute at once the name of Unity and that of Trinity to Him who is above every name and who transcends super-essentially all that exists. In truth neither one, nor three, nor any number could reveal, since It surpasses all reason and all understanding, the mystery of the super-essential Deity." [17]

However, this mystery is the object of the theologian's attempt to arrive at definitions with the aid of analogies that are always inadequate, and yet not without some significance. These analogies may be of various kinds. For, if dogma is necessarily one, theologians may differ through the diversity of the conceptual instruments which they employ. The Church herself has always recognized this. If she has given her preference to the synthesis of St. Thomas, she has never rejected systems like that of St. Bonaventure. The perspective in which the Greek Fathers considered the Trinity is different from that of St. Augustine, which western theology has inherited. The very progress of theology demands in this field a liberty of discussion about the disputed questions, which presupposes variety. It is not even altogether excluded that, at the heart of the tradition of the *theologia perennis,* new syntheses may be composed which put more emphasis, for example, on the perspective of the history of salvation, by using certain categories of modern philosophers of history, or which take advantage of discoveries in the philosophy of the person and the community, in order to deepen the theology of the Mystical Body of Christ.[18]

The theology of the Trinity provides an example of this variety of systematization. St. Augustine starts with the fact that God is mind. But all mind is a principle of immanent acts. It is expressed by an inward word in the perfect image of its thought. Thus there is memory, word, love. So for St. Augustine the unique divine nature, in that it is the nature of a mind and the principle of an act, possesses also memory, word, love. He connects each of these activities with one of the Persons. This shows clearly the spiritual character of generations and divine processions like unity and divinity. But the fact that in God the acts are those of Persons does not appear. Another difficulty is the fact that thought and love, belonging to nature as such, are common to the Three Persons. This is why Eastern theology has always been hostile to this analogy.

Richard of St. Victor starts, on the other hand, with the existence of love in God. God is the fullness of all good things. Love is a good, therefore love exists in God. This is so certain that philosophers have often concluded from it the necessity of creation, in order that God may love another than Himself. The Trinity permits us to understand how love can exist in God, without creation being necessary. God, then, is love. But love presupposes duality of persons, for love is pleasure in another. There, in fact, as we have seen, is the essence of the biblical conception of love, which is the ecstatic conception and is opposed to the physical conception, which is relationship to being and not to person. But nevertheless love tends to communicate itself and find its fullness in this communication. The Spirit, the Third Person, thus expresses the fact that in God there is not only love, but fullness of love.

The Victorian theory has the advantage of putting the emphasis on the connection between the Trinity and the Persons. It is closer to the Eastern tradition than that of Augustine. St. Thomas is to unite the two, by showing that they are complementary. It is certain that all mystery, finding itself irreducible to any analogy, can only be attained by a variety of schemes, of which each disentangles an aspect, and which it is impossible to reduce to unity. This is why the reality of the mystery necessarily bursts through any system in which it is enclosed. It remains true, indeed, that the Victorian theory is also defective, in that on the one hand the unity of nature, contrary to what occurs in St. Augustine's theory, does not appear in all its necessity. It calls forth representations of the Trinity, dear to the last centuries of the Middle Ages, in which the Three Persons are symbolized by three absolutely identical men making different gestures.

A final analogy is one that is suggested by the

great mystic Ruysbroeck. He starts with the idea of life. This is expressed through the alternate movement of rest, ebb and flow, which is, as it were, its heart-beat. This provides an analogy with the Three Persons: "This life dwells always in the Father, flows with the Son, and flows back with the Holy Spirit." [19] This has the advantage of showing how the Trinity is the expression of the intimate life of God, and also of retaining the best of Plotinus' doctrine of emanation and contraction, by purifying it of its cosmological connections. Ruysbroeck retains, moreover, the Augustinian analogy of the Three powers, but at the same time a new touch is added. This gives his theology of the Trinity, as Père Henry has shown, an outstanding fullness.[20]

Thus the living God, One and Triune in His reality, remains shrouded in darkness as with a cloak, even when He is revealed, and enfolded in the cloud of unknowing. Yet at the same time this God One and Three is infinitely close to the soul, closer to her than she is to herself. He dwells through grace in the very substance of the soul, insofar as He performs her divinization. By pure faith, beyond all concepts, the soul seizes Him in His mysterious reality. This seizure of the unknowable God in His hidden reality through the communication which He makes of Himself is the realm of mystical theology, which is a sketch of the beatific vision. It is this final aspect, in which the essence of God—in that of Him which is incommunicable, His holiness—is revealed to the soul in an existential relationship, that still remains to be described.

BIBLIOGRAPHY

A. Gardeil, *Le donné revélé et la théologie,* 1910.

M.-J. Congar, *Théologie, Dictionnaire Théologique Catholique,* xv, col. 341-502.

J. Maritain, *The Degrees of Knowledge,* 1937.

J. Lebreton, *Les Origines du dogme de la Trinité,* 2ᵉ ed., 1928.

6

THE GOD OF *the mystics*

The hidden God of Revelation not only makes Himself known through the evidence He provides in His works, whose meaning is disentangled by speculative theology; He also reveals Himself directly to the soul. He is the "God felt by the heart," whose fire consumed the soul of Pascal during the famous night which he describes. And it was, even then, this God whose presence drew Adam out of himself, at the time of the creation of woman, that mysterious foreshadowing of the creation of the Church; it is He who appeared to Moses in the darkness and fire of Sinai; it is He whose immeasurable weight overwhelmed the heart of Teresa and Xavier, Philip and Francis, Bernard and Dominic; He is the God of the saints and not of the theologians; or rather He is the God at once of the theologians and of the saints, but not merely of the theologians.

However, the theologians explain to us what constitutes the experience of the saints. They tell us that the Trinity, by touching the soul with Its grace, raises her above herself and divinizes her. This makes her share in the love with which God loves Himself, and in the knowledge with which He knows Himself. Spiritual man is endowed with new powers and new senses, which accustom him to this divine darkness, inaccessible to carnal man, and enable him to penetrate deeply into it. These new powers are the theological virtues, the gifts of the Holy Spirit, which enable the soul that has become divine to perceive the things of God. It is this that "eye hath not seen, nor ear heard," but which "God hath prepared for them that love Him" (1 *Cor.*, 2:9). The testimony of those who have thus touched God contains such astonishing evidence that it becomes, even for those who have not shared in it, one of the reasons for believing in God.

The mystical knowledge of God does not arise, like theological knowledge, from the processes of the discursive intellect, illuminated by faith and striving to understand the truths of Revelation. Mystical knowledge differs from theological knowledge, first of all, in its object, which is the Trinity, insofar as the Trinity is present to the soul. This dwelling of God in the soul has its place in the sequence of the *mirabilia Dei,* in the plan of the history of salvation, in the mighty works of the Trinity. It constitutes the very realization of God's plan, the source of filial adoption. Mystical knowledge partakes of the life of the Trinity. It is the realization by man of his deepest being, of what God meant to achieve in creating him. "The glory of God is living man, and the life of man is the vision of God," says St. Irenaeus. So it is by no means a question of an exceptional reality, but on the contrary of the realization by man of his true being.

The starting-point of this mysterious process of grasping God is, then, the coming of the Trinity into the soul at baptism. "If any one love me," said Christ, ". . . we will come to him, and make our abode with him." [1] St. Paul returns on several occasions to the fact that the baptized soul is the Temple of the Holy Spirit.[2] Thus the initiative here rests entirely with God. It is not a question, as in natural "spiritualities," of a seizure by the soul of her own essence through an effort of inwardness, but of awareness of the act of the Trinity in approaching the soul and dwelling in her in a permanent manner. But it is in the Church that the Trinity dwells, and this is why baptism makes the soul the dwelling of the Trinity by incorporating her into the Church. Christian mysticism plunges into the sacramental life, of which it is the unfolding.

We must first show how, under this aspect, baptism is placed in God's plan. The *Book of Genesis* describes the wonders of the first creation. But the Prophetic Books proclaim that God, at the end of time, will undertake a new creation. For the Bible, creation is in the future, even more than in the past. We may say that this is what distinguishes it from the religious books of the pagan peoples.

> *"For behold, I create new heavens
> and a new earth:*
> *And the former things shall not be in
> remembrance, and they shall not
> come upon the heart."* (Isaias,
> 65:17)

We may underline the first words of this text.
Certainly the first creation is an excellent work; but
the new creation will be still more excellent. This
is the very word of the offertory: *"Mirabiliter
condidisti et mirabilius reformasti."* The sun that
shines on the present creation is dazzling; but the
brightness of the sun in the new creation puts it
to darkness.

> *"Thou shalt no more have the sun for
> thy light by day,*
> *Neither shall the brightness of the
> moon enlighten thee:*
> *But the Lord shall be unto thee for
> an everlasting light,*
> *And thy God for thy glory."* (Isaias,
> 60:19)

The Bible recalls the mighty works of God in the
past, only to establish the hope of mightier works
to come. Paradise is not behind us, but before us.
Man in the Bible, writes Jean Héring, is not the
princess sent into exile and pining for return, but
Abraham who sets out toward a far country that
God will show him.

Moreover, the proclamation of the New Testament is that the new creation, foretold by the

Prophets for the end of time, appeared with Jesus Christ: "Today shalt thou be with me in paradise." The whole of the New Testament is in that "Today." It heralds the fact that with Jesus we reach eschatological times. The same Word, who in the beginning proffered the first creation, "by whom all was made," He it is who came in Jesus to lay hold once more on creation and renew it, after it had been corrupted by sin. The Incarnation of the Word is a cosmic act, as important as the creation of the world, more important even, since it is fulfilled in silence, in the deepest darkness. The Word grasps human nature in the Incarnation, and through the Resurrection transfigures it with the divine energies that He bears within Him.

But this re-creation of human nature, first fulfilled substantially in Christ, is continued in the Church; and it is precisely in baptism that it is completed. Christ Himself says to Nicodemus: "Unless a man be born again of water and of the Holy Ghost, he cannot enter into the kingdom of God" (*John*, 3:5). And St. Paul declares, in an extraordinary formulation which echoes *Isaias*: "If then any be in Christ a new creature, the old things are passed away; behold, all things are made new" (II *Cor.*, 5:17). But the gulf between *Isaias* and *Corinthians* is that the former proclaims the new creation as belonging to the future, while the latter shows it to be already fulfilled.

It is St. Paul again who notes the parallel between the new creation and the old: "For God, who commanded the light to shine out of darkness, hath shined in our hearts, to give the light of the knowledge of the glory of God, in the face of Jesus Christ" (II *Cor.*, 4:6). Christ is the sun of the new creation, a sun eternally rising—*Oriens est nomen ejus.* Baptism, which the Ancients called illumination (*phôtismos*), leads us from darkness and ignorance and sin into the light of grace and glory. The Church is the place where the rays that pour from the glorified manhood of the resurrected Christ come to renew our being and make it worthy of the life of a son of God.

But there is more to be said. Up to this point, we have only considered baptism in the sense of a creative event. But what characterizes the sacraments is that they are effective signs; they perform what they signify. There is consequently a relationship between the symbols which they employ and the realities which they accomplish. We must ask ourselves, then, in what respect the baptismal rite signifies a creative act. The essential feature of the rite is the pouring out of water "in the Name of the Father, and of the Son, and of the Holy Ghost." We often interpret the rite as a mere purification; but here again the study of the Bible opens up other horizons to us.

Christ, as we observed earlier, said that "rebirth" was to take place through "water and the Spirit." The connection of water and the Spirit with creation is a central biblical theme, and is allied to the symbolism of water as the principle of fruitfulness. The crucial text here is the second verse of *Genesis:* "The Spirit of God was stirring above the waters." So it is from the primordial waters that the Spirit, who is the life-giving power of God, caused the first creation to arise. Similarly, it is from the baptismal waters that the Spirit is to make the new creature arise. "The primitive water begot life," wrote Tertullian, "in order that we might not be astonished that in baptism the waters are capable of giving life" (*De baptismo,* 2).

But here again, we must follow the stages of development that lead from the primitive creation, issuing from the waters, to the new creation in the baptismal font. This line of development extends through the writings of the Prophets. Ezekiel tells us of the pouring out of water and the Spirit, which was a feature of Messianic times:

> *"And I will pour upon you clean*
> *water . . .*
> *And I will give you a new heart . . .*
> *And I will put my spirit in the midst*
> *of you*
> *And I will cause you to walk in my*
> *commandments"* (Ezek., 36:25-27)

Ezekiel clearly shows us a river of living water springing from the heart of the Temple that is to come.

But this pouring out of water and the Spirit, which is baptism, appears in the New Testament as already fulfilled. It is in this perspective that the baptism of John is placed: "I indeed baptize you in water unto penance . . . he shall baptize you in the Holy Ghost" (*Matt.*, 3:11). Students of exegesis have sought the meaning of the baptism of John, and seen in it the fulfillment of the act foretold by the Prophets.[3] This is its most probable content. It has nothing in common with the legal purifications of Judaism and the baths of initiation of the pagan mysteries.

But, as we have noted, the baptism of John is unfinished. It is a baptism with water, not with the Spirit. It signifies, but it does not perform. It is still a prophetic gesture. The fulfillment of the creative act foretold by the Prophets is to be found in the baptism of Jesus, when the Spirit descends upon the waters. The most reliable reference for this descent of the Spirit upon the waters of Jordan is verse 2 of *Genesis*.[4] As the spirit had aroused the first creation from the primordial waters, so the Spirit arouses from the waters of Jordan the new creation, which is that of the Man-God.

This is how St. Ambrose understands the matter: "Why do you cast yourself upon the waters? We read: 'Let the waters bring forth abundantly the moving creature that hath life.' And living creatures were accordingly brought forth. That took place at the outset of creation. But to you remained the privilege of being born again of water by grace, as the latter begot the life of nature" (*De sacramentis,* III, 3). It is in the baptism of Christ that Christian baptism is instituted. The meaning of the rite is to express the fact that a new creation arises from the baptismal waters under the action of the Spirit, as did the first creation from the primordial waters.

The symbolism of the waters of baptism as a creative principle is therefore solidly based on exegesis, as is all the symbolism of the liturgical tradition. Let us look again at the prayers for the blessing of the waters on Easter Eve. They appear in all their fullness, after what we have said: "O God, whose Spirit was borne on the waters to the ends of the earth, so that even at that time the nature of the waters might conceive a sanctifying virtue, Thou who makest fruitful by a mysterious mingling of Thy power the water prepared to regenerate men, in order that a heavenly race might arise, born again to a new creation . . ."

Thus baptism signifies and performs a new creation. But this creation is that of a new life which is of the Spirit, a life other than the natural life, an altogether divine life. This life of the Spirit conforms us to Christ, in St. Paul's phrase, and makes us His members. And it also makes us children of the Father, by the communication of the grace of filial adoption. So it is a sharing in the life of the Three Persons that baptism communicates, when it is given "in the Name of the Father, and of the Son, and of the Holy Ghost." This meaning of baptism as a sharing in the life of the Trinity is frequently pointed out by the Fathers. Sometimes the emphasis is placed on union with Christ. "Plunged in Christ," writes Cyril of Jerusalem, "and having put on Christ, you become conformed (*symmorphoi*) to Christ. This is why, sharing now in Christ, you are called Christians." [5] Sometimes the water of baptism appears as the sacrament of the Spirit: "The Spirit of God, invisible to every mind, plunges (*baptizei*) in Himself and regenerates at once our body and our soul, with the help of the angels." [6]

Sometimes also it is the whole Trinity who is shown to us as grasping man in baptism and communicating Itself to him. Thus St. Irenaeus writes: "When we are born again by baptism in the Name of the Three Persons, we are enriched in this second birth by the bonds that link God the Father, by means of His Son, with the Holy Spirit. For those who are baptized receive the Spirit of God, which the Son gives them; and the Son takes them and offers them to His Father; and the Father communicates incorruptibility to them." [7] Origen connects the three baptismal immersions with the three days passed by Christ in the tomb, and with the Three Persons of the Trinity, thus bringing out the two-fold symbolism of the three immersions: "Christ rose again from the dead on the third day to enable the saved to be baptized in spirit, soul and body in the Name of the Father, and of the Son, and of the Holy Ghost, who are the Three Days subsisting together eternally for those who are through Them sons of light." [8] For "the Father is light. And in His light, which is the Son, we see the Holy Spirit." [9]

Thus baptism establishes in the soul a new creation, that of grace, which is a sharing in the life of the Trinity. But this new life confers, at the same time, admission to a union with God, "very intimate, mysterious and life-giving," as Scheeben writes.[10] The mystery of grace is the mystery of this intimate, inward life with God. The raising up of our nature has no other goal than to admit us to the kinship of the Father, to the company of the Son, to the communion of the Spirit. It is of this mystery that we shall now speak. It is the mystery of divine adoption: "Wherefore the law was our pedagogue in Christ . . . For you are all the children of God by faith in Christ Jesus . . . Now I say, as long as the heir is a child, he differeth nothing from a servant, though he be lord of all . . . So we also, when we were children, were serving under the elements of the world. But when the fullness of the time was come, God sent his Son, made of a woman, made under the law: That he might redeem them who were under the law: that we might receive the adoption of sons. And because you are sons, God hath sent the Spirit of his Son into your hearts, crying: Abba, Father. Therefore now he is not a servant, but a son. And if a son, an heir also through God." (*Gal.*, 3 :24-4 :7.)

Divine adoption makes us first sons of the Father. It changes the relationship of the Christian with God; it is henceforth the relationship of a son with his father, and no longer that of a slave with his master. The first effect of this adoption is the freedom of the word, *parrhesia,* as the Fathers call it. *Parrhesia* is the privilege of the free citizen, based on his equality with the other citizens, on the sovereign character of the citizen in the democratic city. The Fathers use this phrase to express the state of a child of God in his relationship with his Father. Being the image of God, he possesses a sovereign dignity; and he enjoys in God's sight the right of free speech, which is proper to a son. "Having cast out every foreign element," writes Gregory of Nyssa, "that is, every sin, and having divested herself of shame for her shortcomings, the soul recovers her freedom and assurance. Moreover, this freedom has the likeness of that which has been given us by God since the beginning, and which has been blotted out by the shame of sin" (*P.G.*, xlvi, 101 D). "The human soul manifests her character of regal pride, far removed from all baseness, in that she is free and autonomous, disposing of herself by her own decisions. Is not our soul, moreover, the image of Him who reigns over all?" (*P.G.*, xliv, 136 B).

Such is that "freedom of the sons of God" which a child of God ought to have in his relationship with his Father. "What proof more worthy of belief have we of the fact that Moses achieved perfection, than the fact that he was called the friend of God? . . . For that is really perfection, not to give up a life of sin through fear of punishment, in the manner of slaves, but to fear only one thing, the loss of the divine friendship; to value only one thing, the friendship of God—that is perfection of life" (*P.G.*, xliv, 430 C). "The Lord tells those who appear before God to become gods. Why, says He, do you come before God bowed down with fear, in the manner of a slave, torturing your conscience? Why do you forbid yourself the confidence (*parrhesia*) which is the fruit of the free nature of the soul?" (*P.G.*, xliv, 1180 A).

"God," writes Scheeben, "had raised you above all unthinking creatures. But was it not fitting that you should serve at least the seraphim? God has not assigned this duty to you; your noble freedom has raised you so high that it must not encounter anything created above it. God alone is your master. To Him alone you should cleave with all your strength. But He no longer wishes to treat you as a servant, He wishes to make you a friend. He has given you His own Spirit, that Spirit of which the Apostle says: 'Where the Spirit of the Lord is, there is liberty' (II *Cor.*, 3:17). Our liberty is truly holy and ineffable when we are no longer servants, but the friends of the Lord in all things, when we see the Lord of all things coming to us as if we were His equals, as if we ourselves had the right to draw near to Him with the confidence and liberty of a friend." [11]

The divine adoption already raises us infinitely far above the condition of a servant; it places us in a free state and in a certain equality with God. The divine friendship does this in a still more complete manner. That it may be truly friendship, Our Lord Himself teaches us, when He contrasts the friendship He offers us with the relationship between master and servant: "I will not now call you

servants . . . You are my friends" (*John*, 15:
14-15). "What is more beautiful, what is
greater," writes St. Augustine, "than to become a
friend of God? This dignity surpasses the limitations of human nature. All things serve the Creator. Whilst this is so, the Lord raises the servants
who keep His commandments to a supernatural
glory; He calls them no longer His servants, but
His friends. He treats them in every way as His
friends" (*In Joh.*, X, 13-14). This friendship is
fulfilled in the inwardness that only grace permits,
which is the crown of friendship and consists in
kinship with God. This kinship is Christian prayer.
"Our Father," at the beginning of the Lord's
Prayer, says it all. But it develops with the life of
a son of God until, among the saints, it becomes
that continual conversation, face to face with the
Father, which is Paradise regained.

Grace, by making us sons of God, *i.e.* by
making us children of the Father, establishes our
soul by this very means in a quite special relationship with the only begotten Son of God. Moreover,
it is the property of all that concerns the life of
grace that every relationship with a divine Person
leads necessarily to a relationship with the other
Persons. Thus all that we have said of the filial
spirit applies to the whole Trinity, but is especially fitting in relation to the Father. Similarly,
all we shall say now about conformity to God and
union with Him is true also of the whole Trinity,
but nevertheless it applies more properly to the Son.

This relationship that grace establishes between

the Son of God and ourselves presents two main aspects. It is firstly a conformity, an imitation: "For whom he foreknew, he also predestinated to be made conformable to the image of His Son" (*Rom.*, 8:29). In this sense the Son is the pattern, the example, the archetype, according to whom grace has re-created us. But this imitation of Jesus Christ is not only an external reproduction. "Image of Christ" means something deeper; it is a sharing in the very life of Christ, a transformation into Christ; He is the vine, and we are the branches. So all things should not only be conformed to Christ, but filled with the life of Christ; and, with His life, it is Christ Himself who gives Himself to our souls; He is the bond that He creates between Himself and us, a personal love that joins our souls to Him in a uniquely intimate union.

The life of grace, in making us children of the Father, makes us also brethren of Christ, who must become like Him in all things to deserve the name. The principle of this likeness is given to us in baptism. But the whole Christian life has as its sole object the task of reaching out to all that we are. This is what St. Paul calls "putting on Christ." "My little children," he says elsewhere, "Of whom I am in labor again, until Christ be formed in you" (*Gal.*, 4:19). Christ is born in us at baptism. In each of our souls He must reach His full stature. Thus the whole practice of the Christian life consists in developing in ourselves this resemblance to Christ, in every soul's becoming an image that reproduces the features of Jesus Christ.

"If Christ is Son of God and if you have put on Christ," writes St. John Chrysostom, "having in you the Son and transformed in Him by likeness, you are in some way of His kind, and His relationship to the Father has become yours. There is no longer Jew nor Greek, bond nor free, man nor woman. You are no longer anything but one in Jesus Christ" (*P.G.*, lxv, 656).

The life of grace is, then, a conformity to Christ. But it is not only a question here of an external imitation, but of a sharing in the very life of Christ. Thus Christ is not only the pattern, the archetype according to which we ought to re-form our soul; He is also the source from which alone the life of grace can be unfolded in us.

This is the teaching of St. John and St. Paul. "I am the vine; you are the branches: He that abideth in me, and I in him, the same beareth much fruit: for without me ye can do nothing" (*John*, 15:5). It is He "from whom the whole body, being compacted and fitly joined together, by what every joint supplieth, according to the operation in the measure of every part, maketh increase of the body, unto the edifying of itself in charity" (*Eph.*, 4:16).

The Christian life is not only a life like that of Christ, but it is a life in Christ, according to a phrase dear to St. Paul: "You are all one in Christ Jesus" (*Gal.*, 3:28). Between Christ and Christians, there is a living union. "Since He is in us," writes Gregory of Nyssa, "He receives into Himself all those who are united to Him by com-

munion with His Body, He makes them all members
of His own Body, in such a way that the multitude of members are but one Body. Having thus
joined us to Himself and being united with us, He
makes His own all that is ours" (*P.G.*, xliv,
1317). The Eucharist appears as the privileged
means of union with Christ: "Through a single
Body, His own Body, the only begotten Son blesses
His own faithful ones, making them concorporeal
with Him and among themselves." [12]

But this transformation into Christ, which makes
us children of the Father, is the work of the Holy
Spirit who dwells in us. This is the doctrine of the
divine indwelling. This indwelling, like all that
concerns the action of God in the sanctification of
our souls, is the work of the Holy Trinity as a
whole: "If any one love me . . . we will come
to him, and make our abode with him" (*John*,
14:23). However, the Fathers of the Church
speak most often of the dwelling of the Holy
Spirit in us. The Holy Spirit is indeed essentially
Giving. He is the gift that the Father makes to
the Son. Hence it is natural that it should be under this aspect that the dwelling of God in us is
usually expressed, the more so as this indwelling includes also that of the other two Persons.

This doctrine held an important place in the life
of the first Christians. Thus, in the Discourse
after the Last Supper, we see Our Lord stressing
this at some length: "I will ask the Father, and
he shall give you another Paraclete, that he may
abide with you for ever; the spirit of truth, whom

the world cannot receive, because it seeth him not, nor knoweth him: but you shall know him; because he shall abide with you, and shall be in you" (*John*, 14: 16-17). Similarly in St. Paul: "Know you not that you are the temple of God, and that the Spirit of God dwelleth in you? But if any man violate the temple of God, him shall God destroy; for the temple of God is holy, which you are" (I *Cor.*, 3: 16-17). "What? know you not that your members are the temple of the Holy Ghost who is in you, whom you have from God, and you are not your own?" (I *Cor.*, 6:19). "You are the temple of the living God; as God saith: *I will dwell in them, and walk among them; and I will be their God, and they shall be my people*" (II *Cor.*, 6:16).

This doctrine reappears frequently in the Fathers of the Church. However, we must note here that, in the first centuries, it is rather to the Person of the Word that the attention of Christians is directed. So it is to the Word that Serapion of Thmuys relates the sanctification of the soul of the baptized, although later the liturgy is to attribute it to the sanctifying grace of the Holy Spirit. Similarly, we see Origen and Gregory of Nyssa laying much stress on the indwelling of the Word in the soul. This is the basis of the spiritual theology of Gregory of Nyssa. Christ, present in the soul, sets grace to work—and it is through grace that the soul becomes aware of His presence. It is later, in particular with Cyril of Alexandria in the fifth century, at the time when the doctrine of the Holy Spirit is to be constituted, that we shall see the emphasis laid on the presence of the Holy Spirit. St. Cyril uses it precisely to prove the divinity of the Holy Spirit: "That the Spirit of God is of the same nature as the Father and the Son, no one, if he is of sound mind, could possibly doubt. If he denies it, let him tell us how man can share in the nature of God, by which very means he received the Spirit—how we become Temples of God by receiving the Spirit if He is not God" (*Com. Joh.*, ix, 14-17).

This presence is expounded by Cyril of Alexandria as follows: "It is by receiving the imprint of the Holy Spirit that we are reformed in the image of God . . . But the Holy Spirit is not after the manner of a painter who paints in us the divine essence, as if He were something other than that essence. No, it is not thus that the Holy Spirit makes us like God; it is He Himself who, being God and proceeding from God, is applied like a seal on wax, to the heart of those who receive Him; it is by union with Him and by the likeness thus produced that He brings to life the features of the image of God." On which Père de Regnon rightly comments: "It is the substantial and personal presence of the Holy Spirit which sanctifies us by forming in us His imprint. No doubt habitual grace is not the Holy Spirit, any more than the imprint in the wax is the stamp. But the presence of the stamp is necessary to form the imprint and preserve it." [12a]

We may distinguish two degrees of the presence

of God in the soul. There is first a fundamental manifestation of the Holy Spirit in the essence of the soul since baptism, producing sanctifying grace in her, raising her up by a process which is the effect of a special presence and which would cease with that presence. This presence creates sanctifying grace within the soul, and arouses the virtues of faith and charity. Through these virtues, then, man is capable of turning toward this God who is present in his soul, and of being united with Him through intellect and love. In this there is a second form of presence, but one which is less the presence of God in the soul than the presence of the soul in God, through which the soul turns towards God and possesses Him, enjoys His presence. This constitutes, strictly speaking, the interior life, and in its highest degrees the mystical life. This is that feeling of presence of which Gregory of Nyssa speaks, which does not constitute the presence, but is the result of it, and whose progress he describes through all the gamut of the spiritual senses, from the odor which is the indication of a far-off presence to the very touching of the soul in the darkness of faith.

Mystical knowledge will be, therefore, the hold which consciousness takes on the presence of the Trinity in the center of the soul through the mirror of grace. The great mystics have described that strong and tender attraction by which the Trinity gathers the soul into the innermost place where It dwells. Thus Augustine sets out in search of God, seeking Him first through the visible world, then entering into himself and bestowing himself above his own soul: "There, above my soul, is the House of God. There He dwells. From there He looks at me, governs me, watches over me, draws me, calls me." [13] Thus St. Teresa: "God having introduced the soul into His own dwelling, which represents the summit of the spiritual life, where God is less in the soul than the soul is in God, the Three Persons of the Holy Trinity communicate Themselves to her. This soul sees clearly that They are within her, and in the most inward place, as in a very deep abyss. It is there that she feels herself to be in that divine company." [14]

Doubtless, no one has described better than the great Dominican Tauler this attraction of God who is present in the depths of the soul: "Those who do not take care to preserve this inward nakedness, so that the mysterious foundation of divinity, which desires to reveal and imprint itself on the pit of the soul, cannot do so on account of the images which are there—those are, so to speak, the scullions and helpers in the kitchen. Whoso does not ever go down into that inward pit, to see and taste what is there, shows by this, as Origen says, that he will never be comforted again by God." [15] Thus God is unknown and hidden in us. But seldom does man have the courage to go down so deep, to dig far enough into the pit of his soul, to find the Trinity who dwells there. Seldom does he penetrate this inward sanctuary. Yet it is there that he would find what he is vainly looking for so far away, which is so near—and which would give him happiness.

Can we define any further the nature of this presence, which is the origin of all Christian mysticism? It is clear that there is a universal presence of God in the whole of creation and in the soul. We have said that contact with this presence is a feature of the greatest natural mystics, and springs from cosmic revelation. But here it is a question of something else. Some would place this supernatural presence in the soul through acts of intellect and love, of which God is the object.[16] He would then be present as the beloved in the lover. But we do not see very clearly how love can be the cause of presence. It must be admitted, with Père de la Taille, that there is a presence of God in the very substance of the soul.[17] Intellect and love are not the cause, but the grasping of that presence, which is there before them. God is present in the soul before the soul is present to Him.

Moreover, God is thus present to the soul insofar as He works in her the life of grace, and constitutes her in His image and likeness. This is, in fact, the doctrine common to the great mystical doctors, from Gregory of Nyssa to Augustine and from Ruysbroeck to John of the Cross. God is present to the soul as the actual principle of the supernatural life. "The latter," says Père de la Taille, "over and above the created gift which constitutes it, includes an uncreated gift without which it vanishes."[18] Take away the Holy Spirit, and grace vanishes, which is the odor of God, the ray of His light, the imprint of His character. What is directly, experimentally grasped by the soul is the life of grace. Mystical experience is that life made conscious. But through that life, which is His work and implies His nearness, it is to the very Trinity —without stopping there, it is to the Divine Persons that the soul is joined; it is They who attract it, it is to Them that They cleave. For, unlike the works of God in the natural order, the supernatural works, which are a sharing in the inward life of God, proceed directly from the eternal relationships of the Persons. The generation of the Word in the soul, that perpetual Nativity which Tauler describes after Origen, proceeds from the eternal generation of the Son by the Father. "The gift of counsel," writes Ruysbroeck, "is a stroke in the memory of the man who comes from the eternal generation of the Father, begetting the Son in the height of memory, above reason, in the very essence of the soul." [19] But the Word begotten in her draws the soul towards the Father, bearing it in the eternal movement by which the uncreated Word is wholly related to the Father. The springing up of the spiritual life in the abyss of memory proceeds from the eternal procession of the Holy Spirit.

Thus the soul appears as the image of God in a new and more perfect sense, in that her works have a Trinitarian structure. By this we do not mean simply natural faculties—memory, intellect, and will—but that supernatural image of the eternal relationships of the Persons which are the works of the Trinity in the soul.[20] The soul is caught and carried away beyond herself in the very movement of the life of the Trinity, and through this mirror it is the very Trinity Itself and Its hidden mystery that is related to her in the darkness of faith. The soul experiences, then, in the fullness of its content the meaning of the Word of Christ. "It is eternal life to know you, you and Him who has sent you, Jesus Christ." It is truly eternal life that springs forth in the soul at the touch of the Spirit, and arouses in her that beatifying faith which is already the prelude to the beatific vision.

This has been remarkably expressed by Gregory of Nyssa. He compares the virtues of the soul to the odor in the Canticle: *"Unguentum effusum nomen tuum."* These virtues are the supernatural life. Their presence discloses the presence of the Trinity, as odors that of the Bridegroom. It follows from this—and it is a fact of great importance—that the growth of the knowledge of God, the sense of presence (*aisthèsis parousias* as he writes), will be in proportion to the growth of grace. Insofar as the soul is transformed into God, the presence of God comes nearer, His attraction is more irresistible. The soul then endures impatiently the mirrors and enigmas of which St. Paul speaks, and which are part of our present condition, in the thirst to behold Him face to face.

Gregory of Nyssa has admirably described this despair of the soul in search of God, hoping at first to grasp Him whole and distressed to see Him always slipping between her fingers. But "this veil of sadness is lifted from her when she learns that to press on unceasingly, and never to pause for breath, is truly to enjoy the Beloved, to have the wish of every moment gratified, and to beget the longing for what lies beyond." [21] Thus the soul that grows in the life of grace is always filled by God to the measure of her capacity; but grace, communicating itself to her, enlarges her capacity, and makes her capable of new graces. Mystical experience is thus composed of possession and desire, inwardness and ecstasy. It is, says Gregory, movement and repose, wells of living waters, at once still and springing forth.

This is the same doctrine that we find in St. John of the Cross. No one has laid more stress than he on the fact that in her search for God the soul certainly receives many illuminations and sensations, but that she ought never to be satisfied with this, for it is in the darkness of faith that she reaches God as He is in Himself: "The passing of the soul into the divine union deserves to be called night, because the means or the road by which the soul arrives at this union is faith, dark to the understanding as night." But it is a question of much more than this: "Even if supernatural goods are given to the soul in abundance, she must cast them off in proportion as they come to her. Thus the soul must rest in darkness, like a blind man, leaning on obscure faith, taking it as light and guide, without seeking support in anything else that she understands, tastes, feels, or imagines." [22]

But this obscure grasp of faith becomes more and more penetrating in proportion as the soul is transformed into God by love. Jacques Maritain has well shown how here the experience of St. John of the Cross, referring moreover to St. Thomas, returns to the statement that charity, as it grows, transforms us into God Whom it attains immediately in Himself; and that this spiritualization, becoming more and more perfect, is unable to reach fulfillment without resounding in knowledge. Because the mind is inward to Him, the Holy Spirit uses this loving transformation into God Himself (we become God through participation), uses this supernatural connaturality, as the proper means to a delicious and penetrating knowledge which, in its turn, renders the love of charity as possessive and unitive as is possible here below . . . Thus it is the supernatural love of charity which, by making us enter the inwardness of the Divine Persons, gives faith the power to be penetrating and delicious." [23]

We may notice the primacy which is given here to love. Charity, here below, reaches God as He is in Himself. According to the phrase of all the mystics, charity is a "departure" of the soul from herself. Through her the soul is decentralized from herself, dispossessed, disappropriated. She is related entirely to God, without any glance at herself; and it is this love that she attains as it is in itself, in the ecstasy of the love that ravishes her out of herself, in order to throw her into Him. Here again we must quote John of the Cross, after Gregory of Nyssa: "I went forth crying out towards you, and you were gone. This going forth means leaving oneself, by forgetting and forsaking one-self, which assumes a holy hatred of self, born of the love of God who raises the soul so high that He compels it to leave itself. To sum up, the soul says this: By this stroke that is yours, which has wounded me with love, not only have you with-drawn me from all things, by making me alien to them, but still more you have made me go out of myself and you have raised me to yourself, now that I am withdrawn from all, to join me in yourself." [24]

It is through this love which joins her directly to Him that the soul grasps God in the darkness of faith, while waiting to contemplate Him in the vision of His countenance. This grasping by faith is in proportion to love, for it is love which by trans-forming the soul into God renders His presence always close and His attraction ever more irresisti-ble. The soul is as if consumed in a divine fire of the Spirit, and she persists nevertheless in her difference, which is the condition of her union of love with the Three Persons. Further still, this fire, far from destroying her, renews her life and makes her able to love the more. Thus it is, as we have said, through the growth of the soul in the life of charity, that the Three Persons are thus known by the soul with that obscure and loving knowledge in which knowledge is in proportion to love. This is mystical theology, the royal dawn of the eternal vision.

BIBLIOGRAPHY

A. Gardeil, *La structure de l'âme et l'expérience mystique*, 1927.

J. Marechal, *Etudes sur la psychologie des mystiques*, 1937.

J. Daniélou, *Platonisme et théologie mystique*, 2ᵉ éd., 1954.

A. Stolz, *Théologie de la mystique*, 1947.

notes

THE GOD OF *the religions*

[1] See Joachim Wach, *Types of Religious Experience*, pp. 3-29.

[2] *Acts*, 14: 16-17.

[3] *Traité d'histoire des religions*, p. 145.

[4] *La religion dans son essence et ses manifestations*, (Religion in Essence and Manifestation), Macmillan & Co., New York, p. 157. See the many-sided treatment of the question by a disciple of Fr. Schmidt, Fritz Bornemann, in *P. W. Schmidts Vorlesungen über den Entwickelungsgedanken in der ältesten Religionen, Anthropos*, 1954, pp. 670-682.

[5] *Ps.* 53: 1.

[6] *Gen.* 8: 12.

[7] *Gen.* 5: 24.

[8] See Jean Daniélou, *Les saints païens de l'Ancien Testament*, 1956.

[9] *Acts*, 17: 26-27.

[10] See on this text Bertil Gartner, *The Speech of Paulus to Areopagus and Natural Revelation*, Upsala, 1955.

[11] *Acts*, 14: 15-17.

[12] See P. d'Elia, *Il Concetto di Dio in alcuni antichi testi cinesi, Revista degli Studie orientali*, 1954, p. 128.

[13] *Rom.* 2: 14-15.

[14] *Traité d'histoire des religions*, 1949.

[15] *Hab.* 3: 10-11. See Jean Daniélou, *Essai sur le mystère de l'histoire*, pp. 150-164.

[16] *Loc. cit.*, p. 190.

[17] *I Cor.*, 10:4.

[18] *Eph.*, 2:22.

[19] *Is.*, 40:8.

[20] *Is.*, 55:10-11.

[21] *Treatise on the Divine Names*, i, 6. Cf. chapter 11, note 7 [tr.]

[22] *Loc. cit.*, pp. 560-563.

[23] Mircéa Eliade, *loc. cit.*, p. 366.

[24] *Lettre à un religieux,* pp. 21-33.

[25] See Jean Daniélou, *Essai sur le mystère de l'histoire,* pp. 113-116.

[26] See Hugo Rahner, *Les Mystères chrétiens dans leur interprétation chrétienne,* trans. Fr. Payot, 1953.

[27] *Loc. cit.,* pp. 338-339.

[28] See *Le saint et le yogi,* Etudes, Dec. 1948, p. 301.

[29] See Jacques Maritain, *L'Experience mystique naturelle et le vide,* Etudes carmélitaines, Oct. 1938, pp. 116-139.

[30] See Jean Daniélou, *Platonisme et théologie mystique, 2ᵉ éd.,* pp. 210-215; Charles Boyer, *L'Image de la Trinité dans Saint Augustin,* Gregorianum, 1946, pp. 348-349.

[31] See Charlotte Vaudeville, *Etudes sur les sources et la composition du Ramayana de Tulsi-Das,* 1955.

[32] *Contra Celsum,* viii, 42.

[33] Jean Daniélou, *Les Anges et leur mission,* pp. 25-36.

[34] *Acts,* 11:28.

[35] *Acts,* 17:27.

[36] See G. Quispel, *Gnosis als Weltreligion,* 1953; H. Ch. Puech, *Le Manichéisme,* 1949.

[37] Simone Pètrement, *Le Dualisme dans l'histoire des philosophes et des religions,* p. 12.

THE GOD OF *the philosophers*

[1] Jean Daniélou, *Culture française et mystère,* Esprit, 1941, p. 471 et seq.

[2] *Esprit de la philosophie médiévale, 2ᵉ éd.,* p. 258.

[3] See Gilson, *loc. cit.,* pp. 258-259.

[4] *Life of Moses,* 404 B.

[5] See Jean Daniélou, *Les saints païens de l'Ancien Testament,* p. 126.

[6] Gregory of Nyssa, *Life of Moses,* 377 A.

[7] *Treatise on the Divine Names,* I, 6. It is clear that among these names some are spoken of God literally, others metaphorically. (St. Thomas, *Sum. Theol.,* Iᵃ, *Quest.* 13, *Art.* 3.)

[8] E. Borne, *Le Problème de la philosophie Chrétienne,* Esprit, 1932, p. 337.

[9] D. Parodi, *Du Positivisme à l'Idéalisme,* p. 121.

[10] *Bulletin de la Soc. française de Philos.* Séance du 4 janvier, 1930, *le Problème de Dieu,* p. 26.

[11] I. q. 111, a. 3, ad Iᵘᵐ.

[12] *Loc. cit.,* p. 29.

[13] *Les Degrés du Savoir,* p. 464.

[14] *Loc. cit.,* p. 26.

[15] *Loc. cit.,* p. 462.

[16] P. L. de Grandmaison, *Le Dogme Chrétien*, p. 297.

[17] Iᵃ, q. 14, a. II, ad 2ᵐ.

[18] *Loc. cit.*, p. 298.

[19] Maritain, *loc. cit.*, p. 467.

[20] Gilson, *loc. cit.*, p. 318.

[21] *Loc. cit.*, p. 466.

[22] *Loc. cit.*, p. 458.

[23] Max Scheler, *Formes et nature de la sympathie*, p. 329.

[24] P. de Régnon, *Etudes sur le Dogme de la Trinité*, II, p. 167.

[25] *Ibid.*, p. 224.

[26] J. Maritain, *loc. cit.*, p. 467.

[27] The context sometimes leaves it ambiguous whether by *esprit* we are to understand *mind* or *spirit*. See p. 161, below. [Translator]

[28] *Divine Names*, ix, I ; Gandillac, p. 154.

[29] *La Messe là-bas*, p. 17.

[30] *Conf.* x, 27.

[31] *Lettres à un jeune poète,* 1937, pp. 67-69.

THE GOD OF *the faith*

[1] See Oscar Cullmann, *Christ and Time,* Westminster Press, Philadelphia, 1950. P. 28.

[2] See *Sacramentum Futuri*, pp. 35-94.

[3] *Heb.*, 1:1-2.

[4] *Apoc.*, v, 1-6.

[5] *Foi et mentalité contemporaine, Etudes,* Dec. 1954, p. 295.

[6] *Gen.*, 15:17.

[7] *Ex.*, 24:6-8.

[8] See on this subject Guillet, *Thèmes bibliques,* pp. 38-41.

[9] Jean Guitton, *La Philosophie du témoignage, Cahiers Joseph Lotte,* 1939, pp. 211-215.

[10] "For the Hebrew, truth is not contrasted with error, but with lying." (Guillet, *loc. cit.,* p. 41.)

[11] *Jer.*, 17:5.

[12] *Apoc.*, 3:14. See Vincent Taylor, *The Names of Jesus,* p. 167.

[13] *Ps.*, 31:4.

[14] *Heb.*, 6:17-18. See *Essai sur le mystere de l'histoire,* pp. 331-341.

[15] See Jean Daniélou, *L'Esprit des beatitudes dans la vie d'un militant ouvrier, Masses ouvrières,* Nov. 1955, pp. 39-41.

[16] See Jean Daniélou, *Les Saints païens de l'Ancien Testament,* pp. 115-120.

[17] See Jean Daniélou, *Essai sur le mystère de l'histoire,* pp. 98-100.

[18] *John,* 16:8-10.

[19] *Rom.*, 3:21-24.

[20] *Rom.*, 3:25.

[21] See Descamps, *Les Justes et la justice dans le Nouveau Testament*, p. 305.

[22] See Jean Daniélou, *Sainteté et action temporelle*, pp. 9-12.

[23] See A. Neher, *Amos, introduction à l'étude du prophétisme*, p. 215.

[24] This point is overlooked in Andreas Nygren, *Erôs et Agapè*, Fr. trans., I, 221-272.

[25] J. Guillet, *loc. cit.*, pp. 43-44.

[26] *Osee*, 11 :1.

[27] *Matt.*, 2 :15.

[28] *Is.*, 49 :14-15.

[29] *Osee*, 2 :19-20.

[30] *I John*, 4 :10.

[31] *Rom.*, 5 :8.

[32] It is worth noticing that we find in Greek religion a conception of the "jealousy" of the gods which is sometimes connected with this idea. It consists of the gods taking umbrage at the man who becomes too ambitious. This *hybris* arouses their vengeance. But this has nothing to do with God's jealousy in the biblical sense.

[33] *Ex.*, 20 :4-5.

[34] See Jean Daniélou, *Essai sur le mystère de l'histoire*, pp. 305-320.

[35] See N. H. Snaith, *The Distinctive Ideas of the Old Testament*, pp. 21-50.

[36] *Is.*, 6 :1-5.

[37] *Duino Elegies*, i, 2-3.

[38] See Jean Daniélou, *Jean Chrysostome, homélies sur l'incompréhensibilité de Dieu*, Introduction, pp. 37-41.

[39] *Le Sacré*, p. 38.

[40] *Loc. cit.*, p. 47.

[41] *Is.*, 2 :21.

[42] *Loc. cit.*, p. 84.

[43] *Is.*, 1 :11, 16.

[44] *Mélange théologique*, p. 151.

[45] *Is.*, 6 :5-7.

[46] *Is.*, 6 :6-7.

[47] *Is.*, 26 :9.

[48] *Life of Moses, Sources Chrétiennes, 2ᵉ éd.*, p. 104.

[49] *Ps.*, 31 :20.

[50] Augustine, *Conf.*, x, 27.

[51] *Commentaire sur le Cantique, Patr. Gr.*, xliv, 875 C.

THE GOD OF *Jesus Christ*

[1] *John*, 1 :18.

[2] *Heb.*, 1 :1-2.

[3] *Theological Discourses*, v, 2.

[4] *Adv. haer.*, iv, 38, 3.

[5] *John*, 1:3.

[6] *Heb.*, 1:2.

[7] *Comm. Joh.*, XIII, 46.

[8] R. Bernard, *L'Image de Dieu d'après Saint Athanase*, pp. 22-38; Jean Daniélou, *Platonisme et théologie mystique*, pp. 48-61.

[9] *Dem.*, V, 45.

[10] *Adv. haer.*, IV, 14, 2.

[11] *Adv. haer.*, IV, 14, 3.

[12] *John*, 12:27-28

[13] *John*, 5:20.

[14] *Eph.*, 1:3-6.

[15] *Rom.*, 8:15.

[16] *Rom.*, 6:3.

[17] *Adv. haer.*, IV, 20, 7.

[18] *Matt.*, 5:45.

[19] *Theol. Wört. N.T.*, IV, 89 *et seq.*

[20] *Ecclus.*, 42:15.

[21] *Is.*, 55:10-11.

[22] *Wisdom*, 18:14-16.

[23] *Apoc.*, 19:11-15.

[24] *Heb.*, 4:12.

[25] *I Kings*, 3:1.

[26] *3 Kings*, 4:32.

[27] 8:22-31.

[28] *Wisdom*, 7:25-8:1.

[29] *Col.*, 1:15-16.

[30] *Heb.*, 1:1-3.

[31] *The Names of Jesus*, p. 65.

[32] *Matt.*, 11:27.

[33] *John*, 16:28.

[34] *John*, 5:19.

[35] *John*, 17:21.

[36] See Verbeke, *La Doctrine du Pneuma*, pp. 37 *et seq.*

[37] *Job.*, 34:14-15.

[38] *Ps.*, 104:30.

[39] *La Doctrine du Pneuma*, p. 529.

[40] *Luke*, 1:35.

[41] *Matt.*, 1:18.

[42] *Luke*, 4:1.

[43] *Luke*, 4:18.

[44] *Matt.*, 12:28.

[45] *Acts*, 2:2, 4.

[46] *Rom.*, 8:15.

[47] *I Cor.*, 2:10.

[48] *Origines du dogme de la Trinité*, 1, 523.

THE GOD OF *the church*

[1] See *Ecriture et Tradition, Dieu Vivant*, XXIII, pp. 47 *et seq.*

[2] "The Time of the Church is part of the history of salvation" (p. 491).

[3] See Jean Daniélou, *Essai sur le mystère de l'histoire*, pp. 17-21.

[4] See O. Cullmann, *Les Sacrements dans l'Evangile johannique*, pp. 35 *et seq.*

[5] *Early Christian Creeds*, pp. 25 *et seq.*

[6] *La première confession de foi Chrétienne*, pp. 15 *et seq.*

[7] *Paradosis. Le progrès de l'idée de tradition jusqu' à Saint Irénée*, Rech. Théo. Anc. Méd., 1933, pp. 154-191.

[8] *La tradition des Apôtres chez Saint Irénée*, Rech. Sc. Relig., 1949, pp. 229-270.

[9] Congar, *Théologie, D.T.C.*, p. 452.

[10] See Jean Daniélou, *Bulletin d'histoire des origines chrétiennes*, Rech. Sc. Relig., 1955, pp. 579-581.

[11] This is especially the mistake that Claude Tresmontant makes in his *Essai sur la pensée hébraïque*.

[12] See, as a start in this direction, the works of René Guénon (published in English by Luzac).—Tr.

[13] See the appropriate remarks of Garrigou-Lagrange, *Thomisme, D.T.C.*, 852.

[14] We still find an echo of this in *The Imitation of Christ*.

[15] *Théologie et sainteté, Dieu Vivant*, XII, pp. 18-19.

[16] See Barbel, *Christos Angelos*, pp. 181-269.

[17] *Divine Names*, XIII, 4.

[18] Henri de Lubac, *Catholicisme*, pp. 251-273.

[19] *Miroir du salut éternel*, 17.

[20] *La mystique trinitaire du Bienheureux Jean Ruysbroeck*, R.S.R., 1953, p. 55.

THE GOD OF *the mystics*

[1] *John*, 14:23.

[2] Jean Daniélou, *Le Signe du Temple*, pp. 43-47.

[3] G. W. H. Lampe, *The Seal of the Spirit*, 1951, p. 26.

[4] C. K. Barrett, *The Holy Spirit and the Gospel Tradition*, 1947, p. 39.

[5] *P.G.*, xxxiii, 1088 A.

[6] Didymus, *De Trin.; P.G.*, xxxix, 672 C.

[7] *Dem. Apost.*, 7.

[8] *Com. Math.*, xii, 20.

[9] *Com. Rom.*, v, 8.

[10] *Les Merveilles de la grace divine*, p. 86.

[11] *Les Merveilles de la grace divine,* p. 144.

[12] Cyril of Alexandria, *Com. John,* XI, 11.

[12a] *Etudes sur la Trinité,* iv, 484.

[13] *Enarr. Ps.,* xli, 8.

[14] *Interior Castle,* 7th Mansion.

[15] *Oeuvres complètes,* Tralin, II, p. 52.

[16] See the criticism of this view by Galtier, *L'habitation en nous des Trois Personnes,* p. 161.

[17] *Actuation créée par acte incréée, R.S.R.,* 1928, pp. 258-259.

[18] *Ibid.,* p. 261.

[19] *Royaume des amants de Dieu,* chap. 15; Fr. trans., p. 135.

[20] See C. Boyer, *L'image de la Trinité, synthèse de la pensée augustinienne, Gregorianum,* 1946, pp. 173-199; 333-352.

[21] *Comm. Cant.; P.G.,* xiv, 1037 BC. See Jean Daniélou, *Platonisme et Théologie mystique,* pp. 329 *et seq.*

[22] *The Ascent of Mount Carmel,* II, 7.

[23] *Saint Jean de la Croix, practicien de la contemplation, Etudes Carmélitaines,* Apr. 1931, pp. 94-95.

[24] *Spiritual Canticle,* I, I.

JEAN DANIÉLOU

Jean Daniélou was born in Paris on May 14, 1905. After taking a degree in philology at the Sorbonne, Father Daniélou turned to the Church and the Jesuits. He obtained a doctorate in theology at the Institut Catholique in 1944, and he is today regarded as one of the foremost European Catholic theologians. Father Daniélou is the author of a number of books besides GOD AND THE WAYS OF KNOWING; *among those translated into English are* THE SALVATION OF THE NATIONS, ORIGEN, *and* THE PRESENCE OF GOD.

MERIDIAN BOOKS

Religion (General)

BARTH, KARL *Anselm: Fides Quaerens Intellectum (Faith in Search of Understanding)*. LA39

BOUYER, LOUIS *Newman*. M87

CAMPBELL, JOSEPH *The Hero with a Thousand Faces*. M22

COGLEY, JOHN (ED.) *Religion in America*. M60

DANIÉLOU, JEAN *God and the Ways of Knowing*. M96

D'ARCY, M. C. *The Mind and Heart of Love*. M26

D'ARCY, M. C., GILSON, ETIENNE, ET AL. *St. Augustine: His Age, Life, and Thought*. M51

DAWSON, CHRISTOPHER *Religion and Culture*. M53

DRIVER, S. R. *An Introduction to the Literature of the Old Testament*. MG29

DUPONT-SOMMER, A. *The Essene Writings from Qumran*. MG44

HAZELTON, ROGER (ED.) *Selected Writings of St. Augustine*. LA37

LIETZMANN, HANS *A History of the Early Church, Vol. I*. MG26A

LIETZMANN, HANS *A History of the Early Church, Vol. II*. MG26B

MARITAIN, JACQUES *St. Thomas Aquinas*. M55

MILLER, PERRY *Jonathan Edwards*. M75

PIKE, E. ROYSTON *Encyclopaedia of Religion and Religions*. MG37

REINHOLD, H. A. (ED.) *The Soul Afire*. MG28

SMITH, W. ROBERTSON *The Religion of the Semites*. ML4

UNDERHILL, EVELYN *Mysticism*. MG1

WELLHAUSEN, JULIUS *Prolegomena to the History of Ancient Israel*. MG35

WHITE, VICTOR *God and the Unconscious*. M120

WHITEHEAD, ALFRED NORTH *Religion in the Making*. LA28

WILSON, EDMUND *The Scrolls from the Dead Sea*. M69

Meridian Books are published by The World Publishing Company, Cleveland and New York. For a free Meridian catalogue write to Dept. AM, Meridian Books, 119 West 57th Street, N.Y.

MERIDIAN BOOKS

Of Catholic Interest

Meridian Books are published by The World Publishing Company, Cleveland and New York. For a free Meridian catalogue write to Dept. AM, Meridian Books, 119 West 57th Street, N.Y.

MERIDIAN BOOKS

Philosophy

BABBITT, IRVING *Rousseau and Romanticism.* M3

BOSANQUET, BERNARD *A History of Aesthetic.* MG36

BURKE, KENNETH *A Grammar of Motives* and *A Rhetoric of Motives.* M143

BURNET, JOHN *Early Greek Philosophy.* MG30

CLIVE, GEOFFREY *The Romantic Enlightenment.* M85

COHEN, MORRIS R. *A Preface to Logic.* M32

GUARDINI, ROMANO *The Death of Socrates.* M138

HERBERG, WILL (ED.) *The Writings of Martin Buber.* M29

HUME, DAVID *A Treatise of Human Nature, Book I: Of the Understanding.* M139

HUXLEY, ALDOUS *The Perennial Philosophy.* M144

JAMES, WILLIAM *Essays on Faith and Morals.* M130

JAMES, WILLIAM *Pragmatism.* M16

KAUFMANN, WALTER (ED.) *Existentialism from Dostoevsky to Sartre.* M39

KAUFMANN, WALTER *Nietzsche.* M25

KONVITZ, MILTON R., AND KENNEDY, GAIL (EDS.) *The American Pragmatists.* M105

MARITAIN, JACQUES *Creative Intuition in Art and Poetry.* M8

MARSAK, LEONARD (ED.) *French Philosophers from Descartes to Sartre.* MG40

MILL, JOHN STUART *Utilitarianism, On Liberty, Essay on Bentham.* M140

MOLNAR, THOMAS *The Decline of the Intellectual.* M128

MONTESQUIEU *The Persian Letters.* M104

ORTEGA Y GASSET, JOSÉ *On Love.* M84

ROSS, W. D. *Aristotle.* M65

RUSSELL, BERTRAND *An Outline of Philosophy.* M97

SALOMON, ALBERT *In Praise of Enlightenment.* M137

TAYLOR, A. E. *Plato: The Man and His Work.* MG7

VIGNAUX, PAUL *Philosophy in the Middle Ages.* M81

WOLFSON, HARRY AUSTRYN *The Philosophy of Spinoza.* MG16

ZELLER, EDWARD *Outlines of the History of Greek Philosophy.* M9

ZIMMER, HEINRICH *Philosophies of India.* MG6

Meridian Books are published by The World Publishing Company, Cleveland and New York. For a free Meridian catalogue write to Dept. AM, Meridian Books, 119 West 57th Street, N.Y.